THE END OF THE CONCEPT OF "TIME"!

Book I

Russell Moon

GORDON'S PUBLICATIONS
of BATON ROUGE LOUISIANA
225 262-2581

"GOD CREATES THE UNIVERSE"
Cover illustration by English Impressionist Artist Jeannie Macrae
Of Cornwall England

PRINTED IN THE UNITED STATES

TABLE OF CONTENTS

PLEASE NOTE:

Although this book introduces the most important scientific-religious discovery ever made, it is written so everyone can understand it.

Divided into three parts, PART I: explains why a construction worker went in search of the ultimate secrets of both science and religion.

PART II: EINSTEIN'S MISTAKE, explains what was found, how it was found, and its astonishing implications. No scientific knowledge or mathematical skills are required.

PART III: the third part of this book tells about the search for a proof. Again, no mathematical skills are needed. PART III is also the end of the story.

THE APPENDIX, contains the mathematical proof of this revolutionary new theory. It was written especially for those desiring to see an in-depth analysis of the principles explained in PART II. Three chapters edited out of the original book are also placed here. (Note: if anyone who is not a physicist or a mathematician wants to read through the proof, it should be mentioned that only a High School level of math is needed. Any High School Senior who has taken Trigonometry possesses the ability to understand the proof. No P.H.D. is necessary!)

INTRODUCTION

To all you good friends I will never meet, welcome to the end of the concept of time.

Although it is hard to believe, "time" does not exist and never has! For thousands of years, what man has called "time" is really an illusion. Just like the motion of the revolving Earth was responsible for creating the illusion that everything was revolving around this planet, a symphony of harmonic motions is creating the illusion called "time".

In reality, "time" is actually a function of motion - a phenomenon created by motion and only exists within the minds of men. A revelation possessing profound implications!

If the concept of time were merely a philosophical concept and nothing more, its demise would be a significant event - but not necessarily one possessing Earth-shaking ramifications. Unfortunately, time is much more than just a philosophical concept.

Not only is time an important part of the daily life of the peoples of the modern era, the belief in time is one of the foundations of 20th Century science. Destroy the concept of time and everything based upon it is destroyed too. Because almost every Physics equation used to explain the workings of the universe relies upon the concept of time, most of the 20th Century scientific beliefs about the universe are wiped out!

The first and most obvious to go are the beliefs about space! Because "time" is tied to space, the present belief that time exists as a fourth dimension called "space-time" is found to be totally false. Nothing could be further from the truth!

Although higher dimensions of space are found to exist, the elimination of "space-time" destroys the foundation for Einstein's Theory of Relativity. Even though the phenomenon of relativity is a real effect, it is not being created the way Einstein believed. Instead, it is being created by inter-actions taking place between matter and space that *nobody knew existed until now!*

These inter-actions exist because matter is not constructed the way 20th Century Science presently believes. The real truth of how matter and space are constructed is a fantastic vision - unlike anything anyone has ever imagined before! A vision that suddenly allows us to explain all of the great mysteries of science! From the particle and wave theory of light

v

- and matter - to the unification of the forces of nature, the great dreams of science are finally fulfilled!

But this is just the beginning!

In a stunning surprise nobody ever expected to see, the true vision of matter, space, and time suddenly reveals the actual physical location of the Kingdom of God! For the first "time" in two thousand years, there is scientific proof for the words of Jesus in the *New Testament!* A simply astonishing discovery, one without precedent in human history! But even this discovery pales in insignificance beside what comes next!

What comes next is *truly without precedent* in human history: *has God himself been discovered? See for yourself.*

Because this knowledge is unlike anything anyone has ever encountered before, it creates one of those rare events, a turning point in human development. All science, technology, philosophy, and religion will be forever changed; these changes will radically affect every government, culture, and people of every country in the world. Nothing will ever be the same again!

Although mental revolutions are not as destructive as physical revolutions fought with guns and bullets, they create the same results. They begin new chapters in the history of mankind. A new chapter that begins today with the first publication of this new and revolutionary knowledge!

Because this knowledge is so unlike anything anyone has ever encountered before, it becomes necessary to explain not only what was discovered, but how and why it was discovered too. Therefore, I have recounted to the best of my ability the curious chain of events that set me upon a lifelong quest in search of the ultimate mysteries of science and religion. And as I take pen in hand to tell this story, it is only appropriate to begin by saying I never intended to discover anything. And yet, I must also state that the incredible discoveries contained within this book are not the result of an accident either, I had to find them!

I make this unusual statement because a number of strange incidents in my life compelled me - forced me to go in search of the ultimate mysteries of the universe! Although when these incidents occurred, I did not recognize them as turning points in my life, they changed me, motivated me, and led me to the wonderful discoveries you are about to encounter for yourself.

PROLOGUE

Over the years, I have come to believe that there are two reasons for everything we do in life: the reason and the real reason.

The first indication I had of this cosmic law occurred in 1970. I was in the United States Navy and wanted to join the "Special Forces". I wanted to be a member of the elite UDT, SEAL teams.

While most Americans wanted to avoid the Viet Nam War, I wanted to go. Because I had no religious beliefs then, I wanted to be a soldier. I wanted to fight. And I got my wish!

[But instead of becoming a trained killer of men, I became a soldier in the army of the Lord!]

I trained, got myself in tip-top physical shape, and won two Iron Man contests. Then I passed the very tough running, swimming, and strength tests required for the U.D.T. And later, after passing the physical, psychological tests, and the pressure test in the diving chamber, I was accepted for training over hundreds of other applicants. Because so many applied and so many were turned down, it was a great accomplishment just getting accepted. But it was not meant to be.

During training I injured the hamstring tendon in my right ankle, I could just barely walk, could no longer run, and eventually had to drop out. It was the worst and the best day in my life.

While sitting on my bunk in the barracks and feeling sorry for myself, I saw another former trainee who also had to drop out because of a broken bone in his foot. He was reading a book called *There is a River*, the story of a man named Edgar Cayce.

Because I greatly respected the integrity of this former trainee, and knew he had spent three years in College studying Physics, I was curious why he, a man with considerable scientific training, was reading something about parapsychology - a subject I had no respect for whatsoever.

When I asked him why he was reading it, all he said was, "You've got to read if for yourself!" And so I did.

And after reading about the incredible psychic feats that Edgar Cayce was capable of doing in his self imposed hypnotic trance, I was most impressed. But I took the wrong road.

I became interested in parapsychology instead of religion, and spent four years investigating his phenomenon.

But even though I was on the wrong track, I had broken from the old ways. I was ready to begin my mission in life. Even though my training in the UDT had been short, it was incredibly intense. I was trained how to win, to persevere, and to succeed at all costs.

Little did I know I was about to put this training to use in the greatest quest any man has ever undertaken!

PART I:

Ch1 A STRANGE STORY
IN *READERS DIGEST*

I never intended to discover anything. If anybody had ever told me that one day I would undertake a lifelong quest in search of the ultimate secrets of the universe, I would not have believed them. I certainly would not have believed them if they had told me I would eventually succeed and actually discover the knowledge sought from the beginning of recorded history by the world's greatest philosophers, sages, and scientists. And yet, that is exactly what happened!

It happened because of a mysterious incident that occurred one afternoon many years ago in a small country store in Northern Florida. I use the word "mysterious" because over the years I have come to believe that what happened on that day was meant to happen. That my arrival at the store on that day at that precise moment was not just a coincidence! It was as if destiny had placed the right man, at the right place, at exactly the right moment in human history for whatever consequences await us all.

It all began in the fall of 1974. The energy crisis sweeping across the country hit South Florida like a hurricane and the construction industry suffered greatly. Its timing could not have been worse.

I had just started working for myself in Fort Lauderdale as a sub-contractor in the swimming pool construction business. But when this mini-recession began, people had trouble getting loans to buy pools and I soon found there was very little work here or in any of the surrounding towns. Since I had spent most of my savings getting my business started and no money was coming in, I was going broke fast. So, after carefully considering my options, I decided to leave and look for work elsewhere. For some reason, I had always wanted to go to a town in Northern Florida called Jacksonville. So, I packed my bags and went.

I drove the length of the state, and soon found a tiny apartment on Jacksonville Beach. I got a job on the night shift at a small fiberglass plant, which allowed me to pay my bills and to look for pool construction work during the daytime. However, after personally visiting all of the swimming pool companies in Jacksonville, I learned that pool construction was as slow here as it was in Fort Lauderdale. But that didn't stop me one bit.

Undaunted, I next went to all of the surrounding towns looking for work. And when I didn't find any I tried other towns in other counties too. But no matter how hard I tried, I ended up with the same discouraging results. In one last desperate effort, I drove all the way to Tallahassee – the State Capitol, and spent the day contacting most of the swimming pool construction companies in that area. But it was not meant to be. The construction business was the same everywhere; there was no work available, period.

To say I was disappointed was an understatement. I felt like a fool for having come up here. And that night, as I sat in my hotel room, I wondered why I had ever come to Northern Florida.

The next day I found out.

As I was driving back to Jacksonville, for some unknown reason I decided to abandon the road I had driven the day before and take a more leisurely route through the countryside. Perhaps it was just an impulse on my part, or as others have since suggested – perhaps it was all part of destiny's plan. But for whatever reason, when I was about half way to Jacksonville I turned off of the highway and began to drive along one of those old narrow country roads that crisscross Northern Florida.

Even though this out dated collection of farm roads ran roughly parallel to the direction I wanted to go, after several hours of frustrating driving behind slower moving farm vehicles I began to wonder if my impulse was a wise one.

Thinking that perhaps I was foolish to have taken these slower roads when I might have already gotten to Jacksonville, the sight of a small country store up ahead made me want to stop, get a soda, and take a short break. And that decision changed my life forever!

Just like a plot from a "Twilight Zone" episode, a meeting was about to take place in that little store that will one day effect the lives of everyone upon this planet. A statement which is even harder to believe because nothing about this old dilapidated building seemed important, in fact, just the opposite.

The shingles were coming off of the roof, the long wooden porch running the length of the building was swayed inward, and the small gravel parking lot had deep ruts in it making parking difficult.

When I climbed the front steps they seemed to creak in protest, and when I opened the screen door, the rusty hinges screeched so loudly that I tried to close it as gently as possible to spare the ears of those inside.

But the noise didn't matter. Except for a lone clerk who appeared to be intensely reading something and didn't even look up when I walked in, the store was empty of people. Empty of people yet crammed full of everything else. Crowded into it was anything anybody ever needed. Packed onto the shelves, leaning up against the walls, and hanging from the ceiling were all sorts of farm tools, sacks of feed, work clothes, cans of food, soft drinks, and yellow straw hats. Everything was there, including that which I least expected to find – the keys to unlocking the secrets to the mysteries of the universe. (Quite a place now that I think about it!)

Although 25 years have elapsed since that incident occurred, perhaps its continued clarity is due to the fact that I have never ceased to marvel at the incredible synchronicity of the events that happened on that day. Wondering over and over again what might have happened if I had not taken those particular roads. Or if I had left Tallahassee just five minutes sooner or later, or if there had been no slow moving traffic to delay my arrival at the store until precisely the exact time needed. Repeatedly I have gone through all of the "what ifs" that might have occurred which could have prevented me from walking up to the front of the store and arriving at the cash register, at the exact moment that the young man finished reading the article.

This young man whom I never saw before and never saw again, looked up at me as if seeing me for the first time. He started exclaiming, "I just don't believe it! I just don't believe it!"

Then totally ignoring the money in my hand, he started telling me about the bizarre story he had just read in the *Readers Digest Magazine,* which lay on the counter before us. For no apparent reason at all he started talking to me as if I was an old friend, showing me the article the magazine was opened up to.

Although I listened politely to him, my mind was on getting home. Even though I eventually told him I was going to have to be leaving, he continued to talk to me. He kept talking to me until I decided to leave. He kept talking to me all the way to the door. And as I started to walk out, much to my surprise, he grabbed my arm and insisted I take his copy of the book with me. In fact he almost wouldn't let me out of the door until I accepted the magazine. (I left so quickly I forgot to pay him for the soda, and he forgot to ask me for the money!)

Perhaps he longed to talk to me because I was the only person in the place, or, as mentioned before, perhaps it was all part of destiny's plan. But whatever the reason, I was sufficiently impressed by this man's sincere amazement to read the article myself.

Here it should also be mentioned that even though *Readers Digest* is an excellent magazine, I hardly ever read any magazines at all. I never would have read this magazine and this particular article if it weren't for this man's insistence that it was one of the most incredible stories he had ever read. And he was right.

It was one of the most incredible stories I had ever read too - which is an understatement, for it turned my life upside down. Nothing was ever the same again.

This first of its kind article told about what has since come to be known as a "Near Death Experience" of a man from New York City. It seems that during the course of a heart attack suffered by this man, his conscious mind was not unconscious at all, as one would normally expect. Instead, it appeared to be in another location away from his physical body; a strange location - where he found himself confronted by a grid-like barrier of light - unlike anything he had ever experienced before. But even stranger was the fact that when he was revived, he somehow felt disassociated from his physical body. He felt he was more like an observer, watching what his physical body was doing, rather than being the master of it.

Today, these near death experiences are reported so often they are no longer considered to be unusual or even unique, but, not in 1974. Twenty-five years ago the general public had no knowledge of these incidents whatsoever. So, to read about one of them for the first time was a wonderful - yet puzzling experience. For even though the people whom I showed the article to were delighted by the spiritual implications of consciousness surviving death, at the same time they were baffled and incapable of explaining how such a strange phenomenon could occur. A paranormal phenomenon, which directly contradicted the theory of consciousness as proposed by western medical science. The theory that consciousness is a product of the neuron activity in the brain, and as such, is limited to the cavity of the skull.

Even though I was just as baffled as everyone else, what absolutely fascinated me was the fact that somehow there was a physical change in the location of the perspective through which this individual viewed the world. In other words, this person's conscious perspective of reality changed from the normal position within the body (just behind the eyes) to an abnormal position outside of it - something which is physically impossible according to our present knowledge of anatomy!

"However, the impossible cannot occur, only the possible can occur". Therefore, when the seemingly impossible does occur, it is the signal that mans understanding of himself, is either flawed or incomplete. That a new body of knowledge lies waiting to be discovered, which will revolutionize the way man views himself and his place in the universe.

I must admit that even though at that time in my life I was only vaguely aware of this truism, I was suddenly aware of a deeply felt need to understand, to know just how such an event could occur which directly contradicted everything I believed in. Even now it is hard to explain this feeling, but so great, so overwhelming was this need to understand, that I was unable to think about anything else. For weeks, until I snapped out of it, I considered, rejected, reconsidered, then rejected many exotic electro-biological and psychological explanations.

For example, I thought that it might be possible to create an upward extension of the brain's electromagnetic field away from the body. Or then again, perhaps somehow the unconscious mind of this individual was still active, still alert, and later fooled his conscious mind that wasn't functioning. That he was only imagining everything that happened. Again and again, I tried to come up with a physical explanation until exhausted – I was at last forced to accept the possibility that such a phenomenon could also be explained by the existence of a soul within the human body.

That perhaps the change in the conscious perspective of this individual was caused by a premature release of the soul from the body when the body was in a condition which simulated death. That it was not the consciousness of the physical body that was observing what was occurring, but rather the consciousness of the soul. And that when the physical body was revived, and the soul was somehow drawn back inside, "its" memory of "its" experience was fed into the consciousness of the physical body which now perceived this experience to somehow have been its own!

This hypothesis was a major event in my life. I had been raised as an atheist, and had no religious beliefs, whatsoever. I did not believe in a soul, I did not believe in God, nor did I even consider such beliefs to be worthy of any serious contemplation or speculation.

But now I could no longer ignore what this incident implied. Especially after being trained to use the reasoning process of the "scientific method" – which has as one of its cornerstone postulates the "uncompromisable", unyielding axiom that all possible solutions to a problem must be considered no matter how strange or implausible they may seem to be to the investigator. Looking back in retrospect, it is kind of odd, but it was due to the reasoning process of the scientific method that I was now confronted with the real possibility that the human soul actually existed!

Suddenly, I didn't know what to think anymore.

I was a 25-year-old man who grew up believing that a man was nothing more than a biological accident. He was born, lived, died, and that's all there was. There was nothing more, and those who believed so were only fooling themselves!

It was a tough time; but then it never is an easy time when an individual is rudely confronted with the unsettling probability that his beliefs are a sham, and that his most basic and fundamental thought processes themselves are built upon false premises.

Yet sometimes, what is originally perceived to be a disadvantage can actually be an advantage in disguise!

Sometimes adversity can transform itself into a powerful motivational force, creating an unrelenting mental drive that lifts and propels an individual above and beyond the confines of his former unfortunate predicament. A mental springboard whose impetus gives him a tireless self motivation which drives him, and forces him to achieve much more than he ever could have accomplished when confronted with the mere presence of an ordinary set of circumstances alone. And so it was with me.

My lack of knowledge of the subject of the soul, coupled with an intense need to understand everything about it, and hence fill some sort of emptiness within me, now became the motivating and driving force that compelled me to find out everything I possibly could about it. And I did. I did until a problem developed!

Much to my distress, a terrible emotional conflict began to grow within me. This conflict started out small and then began to grow larger and larger until it consumed my life. It set me upon the lifelong quest that culminated "ironically" in the greatest scientific discovery ever made. I say "ironically", because the conflict within me did not deal with science at all. Strangely enough, it centered itself upon one of the great philosophical mysteries of religion: the location of the Kingdom of God. If the Kingdom of God really exists – WHERE IS IT?

Ch2 WHERE IS THE
KINGDOM OF GOD LOCATED?

The terrible conflict that seethed within me was a conflict many of you may have suffered yourselves. It was a conflict between the vision of the universe containing God, Souls, and the Kingdom of God, and the vision of the universe we see through our mightiest telescopes. A conflict between what can be called the "Religious Vision of the Universe" and the "Scientific Vision of the Universe". A conflict created by the following problem:

When the body dies, and the soul leaves the location of the physical body, it must travel to another location. Or rather, when the soul leaves the co-ordinates occupied by the physical body it once inhabited, it must travel to another set of physical co-ordinates. A set of co-ordinates designating a physical location that has to be *just as real* as the physical location occupied by the soul when the soul was in the physical body.

Since it is assumed this place is a Kingdom of Souls called various names in various religions, one characteristic common to all of these different beliefs is the fact that whatever you choose to call it, this kingdom has to be a real place existing in a real physical location! If not, this Kingdom of Souls is not a real place and doesn't exist. If it doesn't exist, there is a good possibility that neither the soul nor God exists either! And if there are no souls, and if there is no God, religion is a lie! It's as simple as that!

So where is the location of the Kingdom of God?

This problem began to trouble me, which seems odd, because the mystery of the invisibility of the soul didn't seem to bother me at all then (although it did later). At that time in my life I believed in the tentative hypothesis that the soul might exist as some form of "pure energy." Hence, the soul's invisibility would just be a natural consequence of its construction, and this rationalization seemed satisfactory.

But the mystery of the location of the Kingdom of Souls could not be rationalized away. So, much to my own chagrin, every time I found myself wanting to believe in the soul and in God, the mystery of the location of the Kingdom of Souls was always in the way.

Soon, the mystery of the location of the Kingdom of God began to occupy all of my conscious thought. All day long I would find myself thinking about it. The logic of the soul relocating to another position after the death of the physical body was irrefutable. No matter how hard I tried to rationalize it away, I couldn't do it. Nor could I ignore it.

To ignore it meant retreating into a fantasy world where I rejected the great discoveries of Astronomy, something I refused to do. All my life I had been fascinated by Astronomy and the latest discoveries of this subject were still fresh in my mind after having taken the latest college course in it before dropping out of school a year and a half before. So, I was left to suffer with this emotional conflict. I suffered for weeks, until one evening while sitting upon a lounge chair on Jacksonville Beach I could take it no more. Although I liked to sit upon the beach every evening and watch the stars of the night sky slowly appear as the sun set behind me, on this particular occasion I ignored everything and took a hard look at myself instead - and I didn't like what I saw.

It was painful to realize I was going nowhere in life. After spending a hitch in the Navy during the turbulent era of the Viet-Nam War, and after a bad relationship with a girl from South Carolina, all I wanted was to have peace of mind. And for the past year, I thought I had found it.

But nothing lasts forever. The article, my knowledge of the scientific method, and its implications left me deeply troubled. I knew I was going to have to do something about it.

To alleviate the anxiety I was suffering from, I realized I had to start taking some sort of action. So on this particular evening, I deviated from the normal routine. I carried the lounge chair out away from the buildings and the other people. I hauled it all the way across the beach and positioned it down by the water's edge. And as the sun set in the west and the stars began to appear in the east, I decided to begin my quest for answers by defining the exact nature of the problem bothering me. A problem that begins and ends with credibility! For example:

The credibility of any religious belief that includes a kingdom of souls balances precariously upon a believable location for this Kingdom of God, or Heaven. Never before in the history of mankind has the knowledge of the location of the Kingdom of God been more important. Before the Seventeenth Century, this question was not a problem. Since early religions worshipped the Sun, the Moon, and the planets, Heaven was always assumed to be somewhere up in the sky beyond the stars. Since nobody could see beyond the stars, nobody knew what lay beyond them. Hence, this explanation was satisfactory. Because nobody knew what was right, nobody could say what was wrong. Then came the invention of the telescope, and everything changed.

Four hundred years ago, Galileo turned his newly built telescope into the night sky and saw many wonderful sights, but he didn't see the Kingdom of God. This event probably surprised him as well as everyone else of his era - an unforeseen development that eventually presented the leaders of Christianity with a problem. Since everybody knew "Heaven" is above, and now that we have the means to see it, why can't we see it?

Although the priests of later eras were probably bewildered by this continued failure, the atheists were not. They possessed this powerful argument: *"If it is known to those who believe in Heaven that Heaven is above us somewhere up in the sky, and we have looked for it and cannot see it, it must not be there. Conclusion: the Kingdom of God is not real, it doesn't exist!"*

In other words, since the *assumed* location of the Kingdom of God doesn't exist, it was concluded that the Kingdom of God doesn't exist either. A convincing argument, even though it is based upon false logic! But false logic or not, since there is no other knowledge to contradict it, it has become an "acceptable solution" to an unwanted problem. Even though it is based upon a lack of proof, those who use it to justify their refusal to investigate further - accept it as a proof.

The reason why this argument is false is simple. To be able to say something exists is easy, all one needs to have is evidence of its existence. But before one can say that something does *not* exist, one must know everything that does exist everywhere within the universe! The statement that "something does not exist", is provable only by elimination. Elimination that can only be verified by a complete and thorough search of the entire universe! (Note, only after man explored the entire world was he finally able to state that dinosaurs were extinct, and even then, the prehistoric Coelacanth, a fish thought to be extinct for over 70 million years, was discovered in 1938 living in the ocean waters off the coast of Southern Africa.)

Consequently, before any man can state unequivocally, and with absolute certainty, that the Kingdom of Heaven does not exist, he must first explore the entire cosmos before that statement is valid. Without an exploration, such a statement is an erroneous assumption, an illogical opinion. An irrational opinion when one continues to believe it in spite of being made aware of the fact that it is illogical. But it gets worse.

There is another problem that contradicts the above logic! Amazingly enough, the discoveries of 20th Century astronomy now reveal a high probability that the Kingdom of God *does not* reside within the physical universe observable through our telescopes!

This little known possibility must be revealed due to the fact that today, many well educated and highly technically trained people of all different religions are trying to integrate their beliefs with the common beliefs of present day astronomy. Unfortunately, many people have reached the equally invalid conclusion that the physical matter of the universe might block the telescopic vision of the Kingdom of God. Or rather, we might not be able to see the Kingdom of God because something might be in its way, like a dust cloud, or another Galaxy, etc.

Although this argument sounds logical, it is probably wrong due to two reasons: the impermanence of the physical universe - as seen from mans observations; and the permanence of the Kingdom of God - as per the words of Jesus in the NEW TESTAMENT.

The impermanence of the physical universe is now one of the cornerstones of Astronomy. Although we see the same sky Aristotle saw, it is not the permanent place he believed it to be. Everything is in motion. Stars are now known to have life cycles. Some explode into Supernova, and some, like our Sun, will temporarily expand outward. Some day, hopefully far in the future, our Sun will begin to expand until it reaches a tremendous size, becoming a Red Giant millions of miles in diameter, vaporizing Mercury and Venus, while boiling away the Earth's atmosphere and oceans. Turning the Earth into a blackened rock before the cycle is completed and the Sun collapses inward upon itself, becoming a tiny White Dwarf star.

Our Milky Way Galaxy is also in motion. Spinning like a gigantic pinwheel, this massive collection of stars moves through the universe with its companion Galaxies called the Local Group. Its fate is unknown. We know Galaxies collide, and we know Galaxies explode. Will ours? Some Galaxies also appear to have giant Black Holes at their centers, which are gobbling up their stars. Is this any place for the Kingdom of God?

Also, the universe appears to be the result of a cataclysmic explosion called the Big Bang. This belief in the "Big Bang" is backed up by physical evidence. The "residue" of the explosion is seen in the Cosmic Background Radiation, and the fact that all of the Galaxies possess a Red Shift, indicating they are all rushing away from each other.

Furthermore, if there is enough mass in the physical universe, it will end in what has commonly come to be known as the "Big Crunch", to disappear forever, or to begin the cycle all over again in response to the "Oscillating Universe Theory". A situation completely at odds with the words of Jesus, which states the Kingdom of God, will be forever. Which is the primary reason why the Kingdom of God probably does not exist within the physical universe; for how can something be forever amidst this maelstrom of change? It is unlikely. Therefore, it is also unlikely that the Kingdom of God resides within the confines of our physical universe!

This conclusion creates a dilemma. For even though the statement, "The Kingdom of God does not exist" is illogical, and even though it is unlikely that the Kingdom of God exists within the confines of the three dimensional physical universe – what is left? Is there any other place to look?

To one raised in a church environment and trained to believe in Jesus from childhood, such a question does not need to be answered. But to a former atheist raised in a scientific environment, it cannot go unanswered.

The mystery of the location of the Kingdom of God does not have to be solved by the individual who is "trained" to believe in God, because through the generations old process of memorization and recitation, he is literally programmed to believe what others tell him to believe. He is taught (by those who teach him), that those who teach him are teaching him "God's Will", and for him to then question them about where God exists, or where the Kingdom of God exists is to really question his own faith. For him to even ask such a question of them reveals that there is something wrong with his beliefs! (Which is a very clever answer for those who do not have a clue themselves about how to answer such a question and don't want to suffer the embarrassment and loss of credibility - and the challenge to their authority by being unable to answer it.)

Nor does the mystery of the location of the Kingdom of God have to be solved by scientists, because science does not acknowledge the existence of God. Only to a former atheist trained in the principles of the scientific method does it become a problem, a problem that does not go away. A problem that stays with you, and eats out your guts until you have to do something about it.

When I first began to work upon this problem, I did not know if it was solvable. However, the more I thought about this ultimate puzzle of puzzles, this conundrum, the more I began to realize that the Kingdom of God's invisibility might be the solution instead of the problem, because if it cannot be seen, there might be a reason why it cannot be seen. We might be looking for it in the wrong place! For if it really exists, yet doesn't exist within the physical universe, it must be located someplace else; it must exist in another location where it can be just as real as we are, yet remain totally invisible to our eyesight.

Is there such a place? I had to find it. The search for this answer now meant much more to me than just finding the solution to a question and satisfying some intellectual curiosity. It was the search for the purpose and meaning of life itself. For if the soul does indeed exist, and the Kingdom of God is real, then we aren't just a bunch of biological microbes living upon a speck of sand in the middle of a cosmic maelstrom, as some have insisted. Instead, it means that there is a purpose for being alive.

So what is this purpose I asked myself, and what is its importance?

The answer I came up with goes like this: if life has meaning, then the purpose in life is to find that meaning, but if life has no meaning, the search for a meaning gives one the purpose in life they would otherwise not have. So either way, the search for the meaning of life – gives meaning to life.

And as I got up from my lounge chair and stood under the brightening sky that proceeds the dawn, I vowed to give meaning to my life. From that day forward I would have a purpose in life, not just a vain purpose in pursuit of an impossible goal, but a real purpose. To actually succeed, to do what no man had ever done before, to solve the mystery of the invisibility of the soul, and find the actual location of the Kingdom of God.

Although the above statement might sound like some sort of overconfident "bravadoism", one thing I did not lack was confidence. I had supreme confidence in my abilities. A confidence, born of success.

During my military service in the Navy, I was trained to be an electronics cryptographic technician. I was trained to seek solutions to very complicated problems. A job that left me skilled in finding problems in some of the most sophisticated electronics equipment ever developed. Hence, I believed in myself, and I knew that if I could find the solutions to troubles in very complex electrical circuitry, I could also find the solution to the mysterious location of the Kingdom of God.

But I was also a realist. Even though I was confident and full of spit and vinegar, I knew my ability in solving electronics related problems was a direct result of the knowledge I possessed about electronics. While the problem I was now trying to solve required a completely different type of knowledge. What type of knowledge was necessary to solve this seemingly impossible problem of problems?

There was only one solution I could think of: school. Go back to College. There was no other choice.

So in December of 1974, I packed my bags and headed west to California.

Ch3 THE SEARCH FOR
THE KINGDOM OF GOD BEGINS

In order to discover the mysterious location of the Kingdom of God, I realized I needed to do two things: I had to make an overall study of both science and religious philosophy, and I knew I must think differently from everyone else.

Although I wanted to learn what others knew, I did not want to become another victim of their mistakes. Therefore, I didn't want to think like they had thought. The reason why I didn't want to think like others was due to the observation that they had not solved this problem for themselves. Hence, there had to be an error in their way of reasoning. An error that was keeping them from breaking the impasse and making the revolutionary discovery necessary to reveal the truth!

The key to making revolutionary discoveries lies in thinking differently from everybody else. It is not hard to understand that when everyone thinks alike, everyone reasons alike, and everyone comes to the same conclusions. When this erroneous reasoning process is passed on from one generation to the next for countless eons, no progress is ever made. It continues unless the cycle is broken.

I knew the only way to break this constantly repeating cycle, and reach new conclusions nobody has ever considered before, was to throw away the ideas of past generations and begin thinking the thoughts nobody has ever thought of before. Consequently, to think the thoughts no one has ever thought before, I knew I must first examine the facts upon which the current "thought system" of beliefs are based and ignore any opinions of them that others might have. After I had accomplished this goal, I was then going to try to discover if there is an alternative explanation that explains the facts just as well as the explanation which is currently accepted by everyone else.

A good example of the wrong system of thought people can be drawn to and entrapped in for generations, is the vision of the universe where it was once believed the Earth was located at the center of the cosmos. Even though we know today that this idea was totally wrong, it nevertheless survived for thousands of years.

The reason why it survived for thousands of years was due to the fact that each generation continued to reason like the previous one. Each

13

succeeding generation would observe the same motions of the Sun, Moon, Planets, and Stars seen by all previous generations. After seeing what everybody else previously saw, the reasoning processes they inherited caused them to agree with the explanations provided them by their forbears and ruling elite - that everything appeared to be circling the Earth. This idea seemed to be so easily "re-confirmable" for each new generation that came along, that everybody kept on thinking like everyone else before them. Except for a near-contemporary of Aristotle in Athens named Heracleides, who believed the Earth was rotating upon its axis, very few people in history up to and including the era of Copernicus, dared to challenge the explanations provided them and think differently from everybody else.

This type of stereotyped thinking is what I wanted to avoid. So when I finally arrived in California, my mind was made up not only on what to study, but how to study - to study the facts and avoid the conclusions made by everybody else.

Since I had already spent one semester at Orange Coast Junior College in Costa Mesa California after mustering out of the Navy a year and a half before, I decided this was the place to return. So, in January of 1975 I enrolled in the spring semester at Orange Coast Junior College in the town where I had grown up. Since I was a Viet-Nam era Veteran the government paid for my education, and soon I became a professional student; I studied and got paid for it.

Unlike other students, because there was no curriculum given for what I wanted to study, and since I hadn't told anyone what I was doing, I decided to start out by taking courses in Religious Philosophy and Science. Although, I already knew that no school in the world possessed the knowledge of the location of the Kingdom of God, I was hoping to find some sort of clue that might help me in my quest. Since I didn't know where to look, or even what to look for, these courses seemed like as good a starting point as any.

Remembering how a previous course in Astronomy gave me the insight into the impermanence of the universe, and allowed me to realize that the observable universe was no place for the Kingdom of God, I reasoned that other science courses might give me other insights as well. Therefore, while at Orange Coast College, and then later, after graduating and transferring to California State University at Long Beach, I took courses in Geology, Astronomy, Physics, Chemistry, Archaeology, Anthropology, and Calculus.

Unlike the unmotivated years of my youth, because I now had a purpose to study and a reason to learn what I was studying, much to my surprise, I did very well. I got top marks, and was graduated from Orange Coast Junior College with a 4.0 grade point average, which wasn't bad for a kid who barely graduated High School. I also found I liked the academic environment at Cal State Long Beach. I excelled in both Calculus and Physics, finding I had a talent for these subjects. But amidst all this success, I was deeply troubled.

Since I was still caught up in the struggle between the scientific vision of the universe and the religious vision of the universe, my mind continually oscillated back and forth between these two seemingly contrary sets of ideas. So whenever I could, I supplemented my college education by visiting many of the different religious organizations located throughout California. Since I looked at different religions as one might consider different solutions to a mathematical equation, I held no emotional attachments to any religious belief. Therefore, I studied them all.

I studied Hinduism, Buddhism, Taoism, Confucianism, Zoroastroism, Judaism, Christianity, and Islam. I studied the *Upanishads*, the *Tao Da Chang*, the *Batavia Gita*, the *Old Testament*, the *New Testament*, and the *Koran*. I studied the lives of Buddha, Lao Tse, Confucius, Zoroaster, Moses, Jesus, and Mohammed.

I practiced meditation and visited Monasteries and Ashrams. I conferred with all sorts of Priests, Monks, Rabbis, Swamis, and Theologians from practically every sort of religious discipline there was, but I was not at ease. In spite of everything I was doing both in and out of school, I felt I was making no progress towards accomplishing my goal. All I was doing was passing courses, making good grades, and yet somehow feeling empty because of it. The problem of the location of the Kingdom of God still eluded me. I felt deeply frustrated knowing I was no closer to the truth than when I started.

Since I was not at ease, I felt I needed a change. I was tired of living in the city. For some reason I decided I would like to go to Northern California, to the Great Redwood Forest. I had always enjoyed these majestic woods located north of San Francisco and just inland from the Pacific Ocean. As a child, my parents used to take me there upon their yearly vacations. I remembered a magnificent grove of Redwoods called the "Avenue of the Giants" and treasured the peace I felt while standing in the presence of these wise old trees.

So, recalling what happened when I went to Northern Florida and ended up at the little store, I felt some impulse was moving me again. Therefore, I went to the university library, read the brochures on all of the schools in the California State University system and discovered

California State University at Humboldt. A school located in Arcata, a town right in the middle of that beautiful coastal rainforest. Since that seemed to be the school I was looking for, I went back to my lodgings, packed up my bags and headed to Northern California. And just as before, I was right on schedule!

Ch4 HIGHER DIMENSIONAL SPACE

Although California State University at Humboldt is one of the smaller schools in the California State University system, it is one of the most beautiful. Located far up the Northern California coast in the little town of Arcata, it sits right at the edge of a magnificent forest of giant trees. Called the "Backpackers School" because many students go there to study forestry, I myself temporarily considered studying forestry with the goal of becoming a ranger naturalist, something I had always wanted to be as a child.

But that was not meant to be, because that was not the reason why I had come to this school. Fate had other plans for me. I came to this school to take a brand new course just being offered for the first time. A physics course that contained within its curriculum - the solution to the mysterious location of the Kingdom of God!

Of course, I knew none of this. Before I arrived at the school, I had gone through the catalogue and picked out the courses I intended taking. However, I was still curious about the rest of the courses not in the catalogue that were being offered during this particular semester. So as I idly looked through the list that was handed to me at the administration building, my interest in physics made me note the intriguing name of one particular course that I didn't recall seeing in the book: "Space time Physics". Asking about it, I found out that it was a newly developed course being offered for the first time. A course where Einstein's Theory of Relativity would be discussed along with other Physics subjects of current and curious interest. Although this course was not associated with any of the subjects I intended taking, I thought, "What the heck, it's only a two unit course and it won't take up too much of my time, so I might as well try it". So I enrolled, and turned the page and began a new chapter in my life.

This new course was exactly what I had come to college for. It covered many of science's most intriguing ideas, including speculation about higher dimensional space. The theoretical possibility of the existence of fourth, fifth, and sixth etc. dimensions of space; unseen volumes of space existing at ninety degree angles to our own three dimensional universe: other universes!

I was never more alert. Unfortunately, nothing much was known about higher dimensional space at that time, so nothing much was said. Also, the existence of higher dimensional space was not considered to be a serious subject. Since the construction of a fourth dimension made of space alone conflicted with Einstein's fourth dimension made of both space and time, the existence of all higher dimensions made of space alone was considered to be highly unlikely. Hence this subject matter was only briefly mentioned, then passed by - but not by me.

This was the first indication I had that there might actually be a real location for the Kingdom of God outside of the physical universe. So naturally, I decided I needed to learn more about higher dimensional space: and I did. For the next few weeks I totally forgot about school. I researched all of the literature I could find in the school library upon this subject, which was a disappointment, because there wasn't very much available. However, what I did learn was enough.

Roughly speaking, higher dimensional space is another volume of space located outside of our three dimensional universe. This volume of space has a unique perspective: an observer in three-dimensional space cannot see anything that exists in higher dimensional space, however, from higher dimensional space, an observer can see everything that exists in three-dimensional space!

I was fascinated! At last, here was the realistic perspective that fulfils one of mans most universal and widely accepted beliefs about the omnipresent nature and ability of God - from the perspective of higher dimensional space, God can see everything and know everything that happens within our three dimensional universe!

Higher dimensional space also fits the requirements for the location of the Kingdom of God. From higher dimensional space the Kingdom of God can actually exist in a real physical location. (A physical location that is invisible to everyone in three-dimensional space!)

Higher dimensional space is also the perfect location for the soul. If the soul is a higher dimensional creature, even though it is a part of us, it too will be invisible! Although it is hard to believe, the soul can be a billionth of a millimeter away from the geometric center of the physical body, yet never be seen!

I was ecstatic. Higher dimensional space seemed to fit all of the requirements necessary for the existence of God, the Kingdom of God, and the soul. Or rather, to say I was ecstatic was an understatement. I could not express the emotional euphoria I was feeling. To dream the impossible dream of accomplishing the impossible goal is one thing, but to actually come across a possible solution created an emotional rush that flowed like a river of life through my body. Every cell was supercharged with energy. I was reinvigorated, refreshed after the long journey. I felt whole again, strong again.

It was a great time to be alive. Higher dimensional space had to be the location I was looking for, for if it exists, it suddenly provided an explanation for many of the ideas about religious philosophy which were only assumptions a day before. However, the key words are, "If it exists". For in Einstein's vision of the universe there are only three dimensions of space, and one dimension of time. There is no fourth dimension made of just space alone.

Or is there?

How many times in the past have men rejected an idea because it didn't fit in with the popular beliefs of their era? Looking back at history, how many men two thousand years ago would have believed that the world was not flat, or that the world did not have to be supported by something else? Who in those days would have believed the world was really a sphere hurtling through a dark void of unimaginable size? A void so big that if it could be compared to the size of an ocean, the Earth wouldn't even be equivalent to the size of a grain of sand! No, I doubt that anybody then would have believed such a tale. And yet it is true!

So, armed with the knowledge that the true reality is often more bizarre than the reality we envision, I began to spend all of my time examining the unusual qualities and properties of higher dimensional space. In fact, I spent so much time thinking about higher dimensional space, I had to change all of my courses from "credit" to "noncredit" to keep from destroying my grade point average and flunking out of school.

I must admit I was uneasy knowing I was deliberately neglecting the future a college education could provide me with by spending all of my time on this seemingly frivolous pursuit, but all of this extra curricular activity eventually paid off. It paid in a way I would never, ever have anticipated – with a spectacular insight into the words of Jesus in the Gospel of Luke! An insight unlike anything anybody has ever glimpsed before - a revolutionary insight which bridges the gap between science and religion.

It all happened one morning while strolling through the beautiful forest which grows right up to the edge of California State University at Humboldt. For some reason I had decided to take a morning walk. I had walked across the campus, entered the forest, and was following a narrow winding trail weaving in and out beneath the massive trunks of these majestic trees. Although surrounded by the beauty of nature, my mind was elsewhere. As usual I was thinking about higher dimensional space, and on this particular morning I was trying to envision the entrance into and out of higher dimensional space.

The entrance into higher dimensional space is a most unique motion - unlike any other motion in our three dimensional universe. It is difficult to imagine because there is nothing to compare it to. To enter into higher dimensional space, one has to travel at right angles to all three dimensions of space simultaneously! If that doesn't seem to make much sense, the only way to explain this direction is the use of the word "within": within space itself! Or, when matter is used as the reference point, "within" matter itself - in a direction towards the geometric center of matter!

If you seem a little confused, don't feel bad. Since we think and reason in terms of three-dimensional space, higher dimensional space is almost impossible to visualize. This problem occurs because of the way that higher dimensional space is constructed. Higher dimensional space is a volume of space at right angles to the volume of three-dimensional space that we inhabit.

A way to envision the relationship between the different dimensions of space is in the following drawings:

FIGURE 4-1. One-dimensional space consists of one line.

FIGURE 4-2. Two-dimensional space is a plane that is at right angles to the line.

FIGURE 4-3. Three-dimensional space is at right angles to the plane.

FIGURE 4-4. Fourth-dimensional space is at right angles to three-dimensional space. Since fourth-dimensional space is impossible to draw, the following is only a representation, a schematic drawing.

Another way to understand this construction is to look up at a corner of the room you are sitting in. Observe the point where the ceiling and the two walls meet. The ceiling and the two walls represent the three dimensions of space we live in: length, width, and height. Now observe how the ceiling is at right angles to both walls, while both walls are at right angles to the ceiling and the opposite wall. This relationship allows us to observe the fact that each dimension is at right angles to the other two dimensions *simultaneously*.

Although this three-dimensional relationship is easy to see, the relationship between these three lower dimensions and higher dimensional space is not. It is easy to say that the fourth dimension is at right angles to the first three dimensions, and that fifth dimensional space is at right angles to the first four dimensions and so on, but it is impossible to visualize this relationship.

What we can visualize is movement into or out of the fourth dimension. To do this, again look up at the same corner of the room and observe the tiny point where the ceiling and the two walls meet. To reach the fourth dimension we must travel within this point, towards its geometric center, and then outward, into the fourth dimension!

Although this doesn't seem to make too much sense, it does when we realize that every invisible point of space within the room you are sitting in is exactly like the point you are looking at. Hence, to reach higher dimensional space, one has to travel within space itself! Or, since every object is made up of an infinite number of such geometric points, a way to describe the location of higher dimensional space to someone who does not comprehend what you are talking about is to use the word "WITHIN".

As a demonstration, you can hold up a small pebble and say to a group of children that the location of higher dimensional space is "within" this very pebble. However, even though this is a dramatic demonstration, it is a poor illustration. Although what you said was true, the children might misunderstand what you are saying and think that higher dimensional space is located within this particular rock. So an even better way to describe the location of higher dimensional space is to use another illustration. For example, you could say that higher dimensional space was not only within them, it is also within each and every one of us. By using the matter out of which our bodies are constructed as a reference point, we must travel within - within our own selves: towards the geometric center of our own physical body!

Wait a minute! What the Hell! The geometric center! Yes, that's it! The geometric center!!!

Suddenly I halted in the middle of the trail. Desperately, I found myself trying to recall something Jesus said about the Kingdom of God. Could it be possible! Had my thoughts about higher dimensional space revealed a startling revelation? Could there be a connection between the science of physics and the words of Jesus in the NEW TESTAMENT?

The idea seemed too incredible to be true! I wanted to reject it outright and immediately as nothing more than foolish speculation. Yet I seemed to vaguely recall something Jesus said - a quote in the Gospel of LUKE about the location of the Kingdom of God. For no apparent reason at all, this quote just popped into my mind: just as suddenly, I was running down the trail.

I was never a good runner, but on that day I was never so fast. I ran like the wind - back through the woods, across the campus, through the streets of Arcata, on the sidewalks and off, dodging in and out of traffic like a crazed wild man until I finally made it the mile and a half back to my lodgings. With my chest heaving up and down, gasping for breath and the sweat pouring off of me, I finally got the fumbling key into the front door lock, and without bothering to close the door, dashed down the long hallway to my room.

Without stopping I upended and dumped the contents of boxes of books and papers all over the floor in a frantic search for my Bible - which, in my excitement, I forgot was still in the drawer of the nightstand beside the bed. When I remembered, I tore open the drawer, snatched up the Bible and practically ripped out the pages while turning them as rapidly as I could, searching for the quote I was trying to recall. The only quote made by Jesus in the NEW TESTAMENT describing the actual location of the Kingdom of God.

Then suddenly, there it was before me! I stopped turning the pages as my gaze fell upon the red letters of Jesus' quote in Luke 17:20-21. Stunned, I slowly sat down in my little chair. Even though I had read this quote before, I had never understood it. To me, and I know to many others, this quote always seemed to be just another parable referring to the heart or the mind. However, I now knew this wasn't true. Suddenly I knew it meant something more. Something much more!

(Just how much more I had no idea. Little did I know then that this seemingly insignificant little quote is the philosophical key to understanding how the entire physical universe is constructed! Possessing astounding implications, it is the key to unlocking the great scientific secrets of the universe that have mystified the greatest scientists who have ever lived. Secrets such as the particle and wave theory of matter and energy, the unification of the forces of nature, and many, many more!)

Ch5 THE GREATEST STORY THAT'S NEVER BEEN TOLD

When I first read the words of Jesus in the NEW TESTAMENT, there were a number of statements and parables I did not understand. But there were also a few which seemed to be so obvious, no other explanation appeared necessary. One of these was Luke 17:20-21. Since Jesus made so many references to the heart and the mind, this statement just seemed to be another parable referring to these human attributes. In fact, I do not ever recall even questioning this explanation. Nor do I know of anyone else who ever questioned it either.

But now, as I sat in my makeshift room at the old milk factory in Arcata, carefully reading and re-reading LUKE 17:20-21, I realized that this quote did not refer to the heart or mind at all. I knew then it meant something more, something much more, and oddly enough, I found myself scared!

I was scared knowing I, and I alone was privy to the frightening truth that 2000 years ago, Jesus knew more about the construction of the universe than all of the greatest scientists who have ever lived! I use the words "frightening truth", because at that moment in my life I suddenly knew that Jesus possessed knowledge far exceeding anything any man has ever known. How he got it, I did not know. But what I did know was that somehow, he was tuned into a source of knowledge that far surpassed the scientific knowledge of any era in human history including ours.

I say, "tuned into", because he did not get his knowledge from anyone else, "nor" did he get it through experimentation. So what was his source? Was it God? If it was, then without a doubt, Jesus was the Messiah: the messenger of God whose coming to Earth was foretold in the OLD TESTAMENT.

I was overwhelmed. I felt privileged and honored, yet strangely enough, unworthy. At that most precious moment of all moments, all I could think about was all of the bad things I had done in my life. There were so many others in the world who were much more worthy than I. I was disappointed with my failings; I lay back upon my bed weeping and suffering great anguish.

Sometime during that afternoon, I must have fallen asleep. Later, I awoke in the darkness, realizing I was hungry, yet not caring. Instead, I turned on the light, and opened up the Bible just to look again at what now seemed to be the most important of all the quotes made by Jesus in the NEW TESTAMENT. Like a prospector who has just discovered a great diamond hidden in the desert, I had to keep looking at it again and again to make sure it was real, and I wanted to be close to it; to touch it; to hold it; to cherish it.

LUKE 17:20-21

And when he was demanded of the Pharisees, when the kingdom of God should come, he answered and said, **"THE KINGDOM OF GOD COMETH NOT WITH OBSERVATION: NEITHER SHALL THEY SAY, LO HERE! OR LO THERE! FOR BEHOLD. THE KINGDOM OF GOD IS WITHIN YOU!"**

As you read this quote, try to imagine that you are seeing it for the first time. I know for many of you who are Christians it is difficult to ignore the training of a lifetime, but don't cheat yourself. Like everyone else who is not a Christian you also have a right to know the truth.

Although most Christian peoples are trained from early childhood to believe that this statement is a parable or metaphor referring to the heart or mind, is it just a coincidence that it is also an exact description of the location of higher dimensional space? By using physical matter (the physical body) as a reference point, the direction of higher dimensional space (if it exists), is "within", towards the very center of matter itself.

It is also important to understand that if Jesus used another reference point it might cause a conflict. For example, if the physical matter of the Earth, Sun, or Moon was used as a reference, it might create a misunderstanding and lead the listener to believe that the Kingdom of God was located within the center of one of these celestial bodies. Or, if he had held up a stone and said the Kingdom of God was within, people might believe the kingdom was within that very piece of rock.

This word "within" is also a very important word. Even though other words are adequate such as "inward", or "inside", the word "within" does an excellent job of representing both the direction and the location of higher dimensional space. However, as before, the three most important words are "if it exists". For in the present view of the universe with only three dimensions of space and one dimension of time, there is just no room for higher dimensional space. Furthermore, ideas and speculations about the existence of higher dimensional space are legacies of the modern era of mathematics. During the time of Jesus, higher dimensional space was unknown.

But, maybe not to Jesus!

When Luke 17:20-21 is analyzed from the point of view of being a direct answer to a direct question, its implications are too intriguing to ignore. The previous misunderstanding of this quote being a parable referring to the heart or mind is easily understood. Unless one knows something about the geometry of higher dimensional space, this statement appears to be some sort of philosophical reference being made to thoughts or emotions. But this is not so.

To correctly analyze this statement, we must first realize that this quote is a direct answer being made to a direct question. Consequently, it is not a philosophical reference being made to the heart or the mind, or as to how one thinks or feels. Nor is this statement a simile or a metaphor.

To correctly understand this statement, it must be remembered that the Pharisee's believed the Kingdom of God would be an actual kingdom located upon the Earth. A belief contrary to the teachings of Jesus as demonstrated in John 18:36 *"MY KINGDOM IS NOT OF THIS EARTH"*. Consequently, in response to the Pharisee's question, the first words Jesus responds with, *"THE KINGDOM OF GOD COMETH NOT WITH OBSERVATION"*, are referring to this erroneous belief held by the Pharisees, and Jesus' purpose in answering this question is to correct this error.

Jesus then goes on to say, *"NEITHER SHALL THEY SAY, LO HERE, OR LO THERE!"* In other words, the kingdom of God cannot be seen with, or discovered with one's physical eyesight. (Note: the word *"LO"* denotes exclamations of discovery.)

Finally, he ends this statement by boldly stating, *"FOR BEHOLD, THE KINGDOM OF GOD IS WITHIN YOU."* Although this statement is short and simple, it is most profound. If the Kingdom of God cannot be seen with one's physical eyesight, it does not exist within our three dimensional universe! Which means the only place it could exist would be in another dimension of the cosmos.

Because all dimensions are at right angles to each other, the only way to enter the fourth dimension when using matter as a reference point, is to travel at right angles to all three dimensions simultaneously, or "within" - towards the very center of matter itself! The exact direction Jesus is alluding to when he states, *"FOR BEHOLD, THE KINGDOM OF*

GOD IS WITHIN YOU!" He adds special emphasis to this statement by adding the word, *"BEHOLD"*: which means - "look", "see". A word he seldom used except to emphasize an extraordinary statement - a revelation!

Here we must pause and ask ourselves if we are expecting too much of Jesus. The concepts of higher dimensional space belong to Twentieth Century cosmology, not to ancient religious philosophy.

Or do they?

If Jesus was answering an erroneous question with an accurate view of reality, he already knew about higher dimensional space and didn't have to wait for modern man to invent it.

If this analysis is indeed correct, if it is in fact a correct explanation of Luke 17:20-21, its implications leave us stunned! If the Kingdom of God does indeed exist in higher dimensional space, it means that higher dimensional space exists, and if it exists, the present vision of the universe with its three dimensions of space and one dimension of time is in error. Hence, it means that if by using the words of Jesus in the New Testament we can find that error, correct it, and discover the true vision, the course of human history will be altered!

Although Christian peoples already believe that Jesus as the Messiah "knew things no man has ever known", for the first time ever, the rest of the peoples of the world will know it too. They will have scientific proof that Jesus' knowledge of the construction of the universe exceeded and surpassed the knowledge discovered by all of the greatest scientists who have ever lived.

It must also be emphasized that the knowledge of the existence of higher dimensional space is not just any knowledge. It is very difficult - extremely difficult knowledge to obtain. This knowledge stands upon the apex of a pyramid of other scientific discoveries. It is knowledge obtained only by the most precise and exact experimentation.

Even more important, it will soon become apparent that higher dimensional space is not just some mundane, insignificant place. Quite the contrary! Higher dimensional space is the most important place in the cosmos. Without higher dimensional space it will soon be shown that nothing can exist within our three dimensional universe. Without higher dimensional space, we cannot exist!

In knowing all of this, can there then be any doubt that Jesus was the Messiah? Will the attention of the people of the world shift towards this most wonderful man of all men? Can there be any doubt that a renaissance in Christianity will be created?

The stakes are high. Can it be done?

Can the course of human history be altered by one quote from Jesus?
Yes it can, if the error in the scientific vision of the universe can be found.

Ch6 THE FIVE "PIECES" OF THE UNIVERSE

After discovering the correlation between the words of Jesus in the New Testament and the theory of higher dimensional space, school was never the same again.

I knew that if higher dimensional space existed, man's vision of the universe was wrong - Dead Wrong! Furthermore, since the error dealt with the construction of space, there also appeared to be an error in the Theory of Relativity - for it was Albert Einstein who developed the current view of space; A deduction which means trouble! Big trouble!

In the world of science, Albert Einstein has achieved superstar status. An icon of his era, he has a following comparable to that of a cult leader. Even amongst those who have never studied any science whatsoever, the mere mention of the name Einstein conjures up thoughts of great genus and enormous intellect. If science was a religion [and to some it is], Einstein would be one of its greatest saints, and his Theory of Relativity would be one of the favorite chapters in its bible.

Unlike different religions with different sets of beliefs, the same science is believed throughout the world. Almost all scientists, in all cultures and countries accept the Theory of Relativity. Since scientists who believe in Einstein are responsible for training new scientists, nearly all of the scientists in the world end up thinking alike. Consequently, just about every physicist upon this planet sees a mistake in the Theory of Relativity to be a physical impossibility. In every college and university classroom, there is nothing but adulation and praise for Einstein. So unfortunately, within this climate of constant acclaim and approbation for Einstein, for a professor to speculate out loud to his students that Relativity might be wrong, is an act equivalent to the commission of "scientific heresy" in the academic world.

And yet, if higher dimensional space exists, mans current vision of space _is_ wrong. Which means that Einstein is wrong, that his Theory of Relativity is wrong, and that his vision of the universe is wrong. Unfortunately, Einstein's vision of the universe cannot be repaired with a "Band-Aid". The extra dimensions of space cannot just be added to the dimensions that are already there because there is no sound scientific reason for doing so. Such a change would only be a philosophical one. It would be meaningless because it would not be backed up by scientific proof.

So I had a problem, I needed proof.

Without proof, I was painfully aware that the existence of higher dimensional space was nothing but supposition and conjecture. However, what gave me hope was the knowledge that if the location of the Kingdom of God really does exist, it will be a provable scientific fact. It will be provable using the techniques of the scientific method: the same method that was used to develop the current scientific vision of the universe. A vision so formidably ingrained into the minds of the present generation that it could only be changed by the same method that created it.

But where do you begin? How do you challenge a theory that all of the world's teachers believe in and admire? How do you find a fault in the greatest theory in all of science? Not just any theory, but a theory developed by one of the greatest thinkers who ever lived. A thinker, who may just have been the very best of the very best ever!

Wow! Knowing what I was up against gave me no comfort. It wasn't going to be easy. I also knew I wasn't going to get any help. I was convinced of that after casually mentioning to a professor of physics that I believed something appeared to be wrong with Einstein's construction of space.

If you try it yourself, you will probably experience something like this: first, you will be looked at in disbelief; then suspiciously, like you are crazy or on drugs. Then, after a slight pause, you will be rudely told, "What can an undergraduate student [like you] think they can find wrong with the most difficult and complex theory in all of science - a theory that sometimes takes years to fully comprehend. Above all, how could someone like you, with hardly any training in the science of physics, prove what thousands of the most learned physics professors and researchers in the world can't prove"?

[And most amazing of all, this logic sounds perfectly reasonable.]

I knew it was difficult to oppose such a powerful argument as that one and I realized my prospects of finding something wrong with the Theory of Relativity, and discovering the true vision of the universe didn't look too good. I was in a David versus Goliath battle. But David found a way to win, and while thinking about a way to win, I also realized I had one chance too. A slim one, but a real one. I knew from studying history that I needed to find some sort of problem with the current scientific vision of the universe. If I could find such a problem, it would indicate that the present scientific vision of the universe was inadequate. Being inadequate, it would then be apparent to everyone that it needed to be modified or scrapped altogether.

But could I find such a problem? Where should I begin?

Reflecting back upon the chemistry and physics courses I had already taken, I couldn't seem to come up with anything. But this initial failure didn't discourage me. I knew some sort of problem had to be there - there was no doubt about it. Again, if higher dimensional space did indeed exist, then the present scientific vision of the universe had to be wrong. It was just as plain and simple as that. But what was wrong? Even more important, how could I, a lowly student, discover what all of the hundreds of thousands of scientists and professors throughout the academic system of the entire world have not discovered?

While analyzing this problem, I decided that since I did not even know what to look for, my first task was at least to know where to look. So I decided to reduce everything in the universe down into its most basic and fundamental parts. I called this "the scientific vision of the universe" - a term used throughout the remainder of this book - and found that it consisted of only five things: matter, space, time, energy, and the forces of nature.

Next, I reviewed each part individually looking for any sort of problem.

I started with matter. Matter was easy. The science of chemistry has proven that matter is made out of atoms, and atoms are made out of infinitesimally small spherical particles.

Although hundreds of particles are known to exist, atoms are made out of only three of them: protons, electrons, and neutrons. And it now appears that protons and neutrons are made up of three even smaller particles called Quarks. (However, they are theoretical because nobody has ever seen one.)

FIGURE 6-1

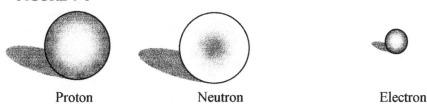

Proton   Neutron   Electron

Protons and neutrons are in the center, or nucleus of the atom, while the electrons are in outer "orbits" or "shells" surrounding the nucleus. The simplest atom, called Hydrogen, has but one proton and one electron.

FIGURE 6-2

HYDROGEN ATOM

Adding more protons, neutrons, and electrons creates larger more massive atoms:

FIGURE 6-3

These atoms possess different physical characteristics and are called elements. Currently there are over one hundred different elements. Although some elements such as gold are usually found in their pure state, other elements like carbon and oxygen combine to form compounds such as carbon dioxide.

Because elements and compounds can be visually seen, I realized I had made the transition from the imperceptible universe to the perceptible universe: a vision I had no problem with. So, I decided to halt my investigations of matter and look at Space. Unfortunately, I failed to grasp the significance of what I had seen while looking at matter.

[It took many years before I was able to comprehend the tremendous importance attached to the spherical shape of protons, electrons, and neutrons. Oddly enough, the spherical shape of subatomic particles is the FIRST of three GREAT CLUES existing in today's mistaken scientific vision of the universe that are needed to discover the wonderful yet shocking truth about how the universe is really constructed!]

I also missed the problem that exists with the 20th Century vision of space.

Here, I knew there was a problem. If higher dimensional space existed, the 20th Century vision of Space *had* to be wrong. But unfortunately, I was unable to figure out what was wrong. All I could say for sure was that the scientific vision of the universe sees Space to be made of nothing. However, how can "nothing" be constructed out of three dimensions of space, and a fourth dimension of "time"! This didn't seem to make any sense at all.

Scientists are supposed to be very pragmatic individuals. And yet, what they are trying to teach us is that "nothing is made of something"?

I knew this contradiction could not be right. But I couldn't do anything about it, because (then) I couldn't come up with any alternative explanation to challenge it. Frustrated by being unable to find the error in something I knew was wrong, I was forced to turn my attention to "Time".

Since Time was considered to be a dimension of space, if higher dimensional space existed, there was probably something wrong with the way this fourth dimension of Time was constructed too. But (then) I couldn't prove this supposition either. Reluctantly, I turned my attention to Energy.

At first I didn't think I would find anything of interest with Energy. In 1976, the current vision of Energy appeared to be straightforward and simple, or so it seemed. Energy is made up of tiny photons, which possess both particle and wave characteristics.

FIGURE 6-4

Photon moving from left to right across page

Thinking about waves, I recalled from physics that even though protons, electrons, and neutrons are particles, they also exhibit wave characteristics too. Because all wave characteristics, such as the waves upon the surface of the ocean, reveal the presence of a medium - the wave characteristics of both matter and energy should be an indication that they are moving within some sort of a medium too; that space should be made of something! But I was told this idea was a mistake.

I was told that the old Aether Theory, which said space is made of something, was supposedly proven wrong around the turn of the century by what has come to be known as the Michelson Morley Experiment. So, I was again confronted with another "dead end". Because my efforts with energy didn't seem to be getting anyplace, I decided to look at the Forces of Nature.

The seemingly mundane Forces of Nature suddenly become interesting subjects of conversation when they are viewed as the "mysterious glue" which holds the matter of the universe together.

There are four forces: Gravity, the Electro-magnetic force, the Strong force, and the Weak force.

Gravity, is the glue that holds planets, stars, solar systems, and Galaxies together; it also keeps us from flying off the surface of the spinning Earth.

FIGURE 6-5

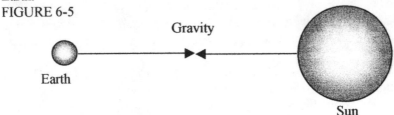

Gravity

Earth

Sun

Gravity is the attraction by one mass to another mass. Since a sphere's center of mass is usually located at its center, the center of the earth attracts the center of the sun, and visa versa.

But who doesn't already know this? The knowledge of the workings of gravity is such common knowledge, and seems to be so well understood by today's scientists, that it appeared to me to be a waste of time to even bother thinking about some sort of error existing here. [But this was a mistake. A great mistake! No scientist living or dead knows the real truth about the force of gravity. The real and undiscovered truth about the force of gravity will shock the world!]

Next, I looked at the Electromagnetic Force. The Electromagnetic Force is the glue that holds protons, electrons, elements, and compounds together. It is divided into two parts: the Electrostatic Force, and the Magnetic Force.

The Electrostatic Force is seen in static electricity and lighting; while the Magnetic Force is associated with magnets. These two facts are also so well known that most of us do not give them a second thought. [Perhaps this is the reason why we do not give two other well-known facts about these forces a second thought either; two facts that are vitally important. Two facts that are really the SECOND and THIRD GREAT CLUES needed to discover the true vision of the universe:]

FIGURE 6-6

Electron

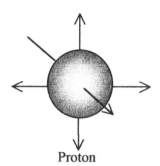

Proton

[FACT #1 Note how the lines that represent the electrostatic force point *directly into or out of the geometric center* of each "particle." Although this simple observation doesn't seem to be of any importance whatsoever, it is the *SECOND GREAT CLUE* to deciphering the true nature of how the universe is constructed.]

[FACT #2 Now take another look at the magnetic force drawn below. Although most of us can remember seeing pictures of the lines of electromagnetic flux surrounding bar magnets, note the curious way they *resemble currents flowing into and out of* the metallic bar. This extremely important observation is the THIRD GREAT CLUE needed to deduce the true vision of the universe.]

FIGURE 6-7

And last but not least, there is the Strong and Weak Forces. These two forces are the glue and "non-glue" associated mainly with the center or nucleus of atoms. The strong force holds protons and neutrons together, while the weak force is responsible for the unusual phenomenon associated with the break-up of neutrons:

FIGURE 6-8

Strong Force   Strong Force

Proton Neutron

[Again, observe how the strong force is somehow concentrated at the center of each particle.]

FIGURE 6-9

1

proton   electron   gamma ray

Neutron.

Weak Force begins
breakup of neutron.

Neutron breaks up into
a proton, an electron,
and a gamma ray.

[Note how the break up of a neutron into a proton, an electron, and a gamma ray (powerful Photon of light) almost makes it look as if the neutron is somehow made up of a proton and an electron?]

But again, just like matter, space, time, and energy, I could find nothing wrong with the forces of nature. It was terribly frustrating. Everything I looked at seemed to be perfectly normal. But I knew it could not be right. If higher dimensional space really existed, something had to be wrong someplace!

note: Typographical error, the word anti-
neutrino should be substituted for the word
gamma ray in the above description.

Ch7 HARD TIMES

Identifying a problem is one thing, solving it is another.

Although I wanted to believe higher dimensional space existed, I knew I could not believe in it until I could prove it scientifically. But to prove it scientifically I had to find the mistake in the present scientific vision of the universe. This mistake had to be a major one, a mistake of enormous proportions. But at the moment, this mistake eluded me, and my failure to find it frustrated me to no end.

This frustration created a great deal of stress. The search for the mistake in the scientific vision of the universe was now one of the great quests in my life, but I was also a realist. I knew it might take years of schooling before I was able to discover this mistake, and as mentioned before, I had no illusions about getting any help from Physicists.

It was a tough time. I didn't know what to do. I only knew I wanted to learn the truth, and I now knew I could not learn the truth in school. This attitude made it hard to sit in class anymore.

Being absolutely certain that a great error of enormous proportions existed somewhere in the scientific vision of the universe; it was hard to take seriously any of the science courses I was enrolled in. Nor could I fool myself! If higher dimensional space existed, some, most, or all of what I was being taught was wrong. This realization created a pessimistic attitude I couldn't shake. I became disenchanted with the scientific world. I came to school to find the truth, and now, as I sat in class and looked disappointedly around the room, I became disillusioned. I realized that many of the people who were here could care less about the truth.

The professor who was teaching the course was making a paycheck. He was earning a living teaching others what he had been taught. If he was wrong, what the hell, he still got paid!

Most of the students were also a disappointment. They were here because they had to be here. Many of these science courses were required courses they needed to take to complete their college education and get their diplomas. They were merely doing what they had to, to graduate.

As we used to say in the 60s, "It was a downer!" The learning technique was also a disappointment. Students would sit in class writing down, without question or complaint, whatever was said. Then they would go home, study it, and memorize it to be able to pass the tests and get through the course.

What was even more painful was the realization that I was no better than the rest. I had fallen into the same trap myself. All I seemed to be doing was sitting in class, taking notes, and passing tests.

I also realized that any students who had the nerve to stand up and speak out never got the chance. So much knowledge is thrown at students in such a short period of time, there is no time for the "intellectual digestion processes" to take place. There was hardly any time for introspection and contemplation. The mind was never given the opportunity to sift through all of this new information and look for errors.

Inevitably, I became disenchanted with the academic experience.

I also went kind of crazy.

After the experience of the store in Florida, and the transfer to the University in Arcata, I now believed in the concept of "synchronicity". I believed that all a person had to do to succeed, was to hold a goal within their mind and wait to be guided into those particular circumstances where the solution would be found. But, I was impatient.

Although I believe in this mental process today, and know it to be absolutely true, at that time in my life I did not know *how* it worked. All I knew then was that impulsive actions seemed to play a greater role in my life than the carefully thought out ones. Impulsive actions seemed to be the actions that guided me to the circumstances where the solution was waiting to be found. However, in attempting to force this process to occur, I ended up going off on a weird odyssey.

Every time I had an impulse to do something, I did it.

One day I thought I would like to go backpacking. Then I thought that if I wanted to go backpacking, perhaps I needed to. Perhaps at the end of the trail I would find the answer I was looking for. So, I purchased a backpack, bought rice, beans, and a few cans of corned beef, and headed down the road. Just headed down the road not having the slightest idea where I was going or where I would end up. Since circumstance eventually led me to a small town in Northern California called Paradise, I thought this was where my next residence was meant to be. Perhaps this was where the answer I was looking for awaited me? So after returning for the final few weeks of the semester at Humboldt, I quit school and went to Paradise.

Because of my religious investigations, I was enchanted with the name "Paradise". An enchantment that soon ended when to my dismay, I learned the town was originally called "Pair of Dice". A name given to it because of all the riotous gambling which took place there during the

19th Century Gold Rush. So as suddenly as I became interested, I lost interest in that name. However, because this town was located near another town called Chico, which just happened to have another branch of the California State University system located there, I thought that this must have been the reason why I ended up in Paradise.

So I enrolled. I changed my major to Civil Engineering and spent a semester there.

But if I was disenchanted with school before, I was really disenchanted now. I did not know that Chico was notorious for being a "party" school where fraternity and sorority groups dominate the town. It was disgusting to see these young adults seeking to fit in with the expectations of their peer groups rather than seeking to develop their own individualities. They were like plastic people being pressed into lookalike molds. Disappointed, I felt another change was needed – this time in "ME".

Reluctantly, I gave up looking for the hidden meanings of life in every move I made. Dejected, I left Chico and at the end of another long odyssey, finally ended up going back to California State University at Long Beach. But even though I tried to again force myself to study with the same intensity I did when I was there before, it was no good.

The past eventually caught up with me again. Having to take Third Semester Physics as part of my Civil Engineering requirements, I rebelled. Third Semester Physics deals mainly with Einstein's vision of the universe and his Theory of Relativity. Two subjects I knew for sure had to contain major errors.

For weeks I sat in class, discontented. The evidence for the acceptance of the Theory was very impressive. I reluctantly listened as the professor said; "Einstein's brilliant deduction of the fourth dimension of space-time explains many of the unusual phenomenon of the universe. For example, this fourth dimension of time is responsible for the length shrinkage and time dilation effects which occur at near light velocities." (Of course I did not know then that there is no fourth dimension of "space-time." Even though there is a fourth dimension, a structure within the atom that nobody knew existed is responsible for these length shrinkage and time dilation effects).

He then went on to say, "Further proof of the Theory of Relativity is found in the observations of very fast moving subatomic particles. The disintegration of fast moving subatomic particles acts in perfect accordance with the Theory of Relativity. When short lived particles such as the Muon (a heavier version of the electron) are moving faster, they exist for longer periods of time before disintegrating into smaller particles" (I also did not know then that there is a completely different explanation for this phenomenon).

He went on to mention that another proof of Relativity was seen in an experiment done with an atomic clock.

An atomic clock launched into space and orbiting the earth at twenty five thousand miles an hour runs slower than a clock located down here with us. And he concluded by saying, "This slowing down of an atomic clock located within a satellite orbiting the Earth is a further confirmation of Mr. Einstein's famous theory." (A statement that is totally and completely wrong! This phenomenon is not a confirmation of the Theory of Relativity at all! Later, it will be shown that this effect is also being created by unforeseen and unsuspected structures existing within the atom.) However, I did not know then the knowledge within the above parenthesis.

All I knew in 1978 was that when these observations are added to Einstein's use of Relativity to explain some unusual motions in the orbit of the planet Mercury, I myself had to confess that this was some pretty impressive evidence. It was extremely hard for me then to deny science's conclusion: "that the Theory of Relativity is true, is proven true, and there is nothing more to say!" (It was only much later that I learned there *is* indeed a lot more to say - much more!)

But in 1978, to say I was discouraged was an understatement. After hearing all of these unbreakable affirmations for which I possessed no alternative explanations, I was deeply troubled. How could all of this evidence possibly be wrong? If only Einstein's fourth dimension of time didn't exist, there would not be a barrier between the three lower dimensions of space and higher dimensions of space. Everything would be fine. But it was there, and it seemed to account for many of the strange time dilation phenomenon that are observed to exist at near light velocities. The evidence seemed overwhelming. And I was worn out.

I didn't believe Einstein was right and I couldn't prove him wrong. I refused to learn what was being taught. And by refusing to learn I couldn't pass tests.

With this rebellious attitude, no matter how hard I tried to fit in and be a part of the academic system, it didn't work. It was only with great difficulty that I picked up the books I no longer cared about and forced myself to study.

Eventually, I knew I had to go. One day, I just got up and walked out. I stood up, right in the middle of class, and with everybody watching me, gathered up my books, walked across the classroom to the door, opened it, and walked out of the academic world forever.

I must admit I was sorry to go. Not because I was sorry to leave that environment, but rather, because I felt I was a complete failure. I had failed to learn where the error in science existed. I wanted to use the principles of science to prove that higher dimensional space existed but I was unable to do that too. And lastly, I believed I had failed to acquire the knowledge or the skills necessary to accomplish either of the above goals. Hence I was depressed. [Not knowing then, that I had already acquired the knowledge and the mathematical skills necessary to prove the Theory of Relativity was wrong. That another theory about the construction of the universe was waiting to be discovered that would revolutionize science, and prove that Jesus' location for the Kingdom of God actually exists!]

But the proof had to wait for many years because I was not well.

Considering the last four years of my life to be an utter waste of time, I had no idea what to do. For a while, I just drifted around. In a kind of "purposeless wandering", I drove all over Northern California and Oregon. I had no idea where to go. Life had no meaning. I did odd jobs to make enough money for gas and food and I slept in my car. When I eventually returned to Southern California to search for a more lasting job, I tried to forget about everything.

I wanted to forget about science, higher dimensional space, and get the problem of the location of the Kingdom of God out of my mind forever. I tried to forget about trying to find a way to prove the existence of anything. I was sorry I had ever even heard about the Theory of Relativity, but the rejection never worked.

Eventually I found myself thinking about the problem all over again, and I wasn't able to concentrate upon anything else. Since I never told anybody what I was doing, most of the people who knew me thought I was nuts. Perhaps I was!

Because of this stress, I couldn't stand to be any one place too long. I would get a job, work for awhile then quit and move on. I was never satisfied with anything I did. I traveled all over the southwestern United States. But eventually, my wanderings found me back in Florida, where, after a number of years, I became a State Licensed Commercial Swimming Pool Contractor. I built pools, or worked as a superintendent for other builders.

Without going into details, suffice it to say, many years passed and many events occurred. But even though I tried desperately to avoid it, every once in a while I would start thinking about the error in science and my failure to prove the existence of the Kingdom of God. Then, just like a soldier suffering from some sort of Post-Traumatic Stress Syndrome, I would have flashbacks, and suffer terrible feelings of stress and anxiety that sometimes lasted for weeks. While in the interim, I tried my best to cope, to get by and to live with a sense of failure.

And then one afternoon, everything changed. Mediocrity disappeared - exhilaration returned! In a flash of inspiration I was finally able to deduce the great error which exists in Einstein's Theory of Relativity – the error that allowed me to discover the true vision of the universe; a stunning, spectacular vision no man has ever seen before! A vision of the universe that allowed me to explain all of the great mysteries of science!

But most important of all, after what seemed like a lifetime of suffering, I was able to scientifically prove that Jesus' location for the Kingdom of God actually exists! (And an even more shocking revelation about God!)

It happened like this...

PART II

Ch8 EINSTEIN'S MISTAKE

1989 was a good year.

I told myself the stresses of the past were gone and I was content living a life free of the need to discover the mistake in the scientific vision of the universe. Leave that to others; I was happy in being happy, and wanted nothing else. I was making money, and doing the kind of work I enjoyed doing. I had no problems and wanted none.

Then one day the past caught up with me. Everything changed. In one hour my happy though meaningless little existence was blown away. Because of that day, nothing will ever be the same again for any of us. For on that day the great error in Einstein's vision of the universe was deduced.

It all happened one particularly hot and humid afternoon in Margate, a suburb of Fort Lauderdale. I was working as a swimming pool subcontractor; building homeowner pools for a now defunct company called Swimming Pool World. Working for myself and by myself, I would lay out the shape of the pool, supervise the digging of the hole, form the shape of the pool out of wood, and then finally install the reinforcing bar.

In the winter, the weather was not bad for this kind of work. But in the summer, it got hot and humid down in those holes. And on this particular day, it was hot, real hot!

It was so hot that I could only work for a little while in the hole, then I had to climb out, turn on the hose, douse myself with water, and go sit for awhile in the shade of a tree.

Like other construction workers, I had no choice but to work in the intense summer heat of Florida. But to beat the effects of the heat, I had developed the technique of intensely concentrating upon a philosophical problem. I found when I did this the resulting introspection effectively removed my conscious mind from its unpleasant surroundings. These mental gymnastics allowed me to keep working where others couldn't. Although in the past I thought about a variety of subjects, on this particular day, I was thinking about "time".

Time has always held a fascination for me. Many years before when looking for the error in Einstein's vision of the universe, I had researched the origins of time. Or rather, I had tried to research the origins of time. Although there are a number of books written upon the concept of time, they are incomplete. The concept of time is an ancient concept so old its origins are lost in antiquity.

The early civilizations that documented the concept of time were chronicling a concept created much earlier than the creation of writing. (Note: this idea is not speculation. In 1993, it was reported in *SMITHSONIAN TIMELINES OF THE ANCIENT WORLD* [see REFERENCES], that a carved bone discovered in the Grotto du Tai in France appears to be a solar calendar dating back to 10,000 BC.)

The important point to remember about the concept of time is that it was developed during an era of great ignorance. The concept of time was developed during a period when man knew nothing about the motions of the Earth, Moon, Planets, or Sun, which is ironic because these motions are, and always have been associated with the passage of time! For example, the day is one rotation of the Earth upon its axis, the month is approximately one orbit of the Moon around the Earth, and the year is one orbit of the Earth around the Sun.

In fact, since all motion is associated with time, on this particular day, I began to wonder about just what motion it was that brought about mans first perception of this most enduring of all ideas?

Naturally, I began by telling myself that since both the "day" and the "year" are two important lengths of time associated with celestial motions, the first perception of time probably began with early mans most rudimentary astronomical observations.

Almost everybody could see that day followed night and night followed day. The Sun, Moon, and stars rose above the eastern horizon and set below the western horizon. This entire phenomenon was visible for everyone to observe. However, a very clever individual would have begun to notice an unwavering regularity in these motions and would probably have begun to keep track of them through association with other motions.

Noting the phases of the Moon, he might realize that if he made one mark upon an object for each day of the lunar cycle, he would discover that this constantly repeating light show always occurred during the same number of days. He would also observe the night sky, and notice how various star patterns would either disappear or reappear during different seasons of the year. And if he were lucky enough to live in one small geographical location year in and year out, he would notice how the location of the rising Sun continually changes its position each day.

Slowly trudging northward for six months, stopping, then heading southward for six months, stopping, then repeating the whole process over and over again, year after unbroken year. Although this particular phenomenon was probably noticed only by later agrarian societies, which tended to live more stationary lives in contrast to the wanderings of the early hunter, gatherer groups.

I was about to continue on with these mental speculations when I was suddenly halted by an astounding idea I never thought before - was dawn age man really sophisticated enough to recognize such an abstract concept as time?

The concept of time is a very abstract idea. It cannot be perceived with the senses. It can only be deduced through observations associated with motion. This observation is extremely important, for many of our conclusions are based upon our perceptions, but sometimes our perceptions are based upon our conceptions.

Consequently, was dawn age man cognizant enough of his mental processes to differentiate between the two? [Is anybody?] Spoken more bluntly, did he perceive time, or did he conceive time?

When considering this hypothesis, we tend to forget that the concept of time is not a concept that we as 20th century men developed. It is a mental legacy inherited from early man, and passed on from generation to generation. A concept developed within the reasoning process of the child like superstitious minds of our ancient ancestors - men that were totally ignorant of the astronomical knowledge we take for granted today.

Today, it is hard for many of us to accept the fact that grammar school children know more about the motions of the Earth and the solar system than the greatest philosophers in the Golden age of Greece. It is hard to believe that six and seven-year-old kids know more about the orbits of the planets than Plato, Socrates, or Aristotle! But what is really astounding, is that these men knew far more than their ancient forbears did who were responsible for developing the concept of time!

Since the workings of the solar system are so obvious to us, it is hard for us to envision a time when men knew nothing about the motions of the Earth. It is also easy for us to forget today that ancient peoples did not know the Earth was rotating - creating the effect that everything was circling it. Or that the changing location of the Earth in its orbit around the Sun was responsible for making different star constellations appear at different seasons of the year; or that during its orbit of the Sun, the Earth's 23.5 degree tilt was creating the four seasons.

In fact, everything ancient peoples were observing in the sky were actually effects being created by motions they were totally unaware of.

It gets even more uncomfortable when we realize our concept of time was developed by men who worshipped fire, feared thunder and lighting as the wrath of the gods, and made animal sacrifices for good crops and successful hunts.

In all honesty, I must admit that I was surprised to find myself even thinking these thoughts I had never thought of before. I found myself wondering if anyone else had ever thought like this before? The concept of time is so much a part of our daily lives that to question its validity, even within the privacy of our own thoughts seems ludicrous - if not insanity itself.

But then, "just because" everyone "knows" time exists, doesn't mean it does. Once upon a time everyone "knew" the world was flat, everyone "knew" the Earth was at the center of the universe, and everyone "knew" that Aristotle's vision of an unchanging universe was absolutely correct. Once, to be a member of the educated elite, everyone studied Aristotle and knew that the stars were in stationary positions in the night sky. The so-called "educated people" "knew" the positions of the stars were eternal and unchanging. But what is most disconcerting of all, is the fact that all of these totally false and erroneous ideas endured from generation to generation for almost two thousand of years!

Man has grown comfortable with his belief in time. But suddenly I wasn't. I began to suspect that the concept of time might be nothing less than a total and complete mistake! Perhaps the greatest blunder mankind has ever made!

Although the concept of time might have started out as a simple concept, in the 20th Century it has become extremely abstract. A situation which causes it to be suspect. I have learned from my analysis of previous erroneous ideas, such as ancient mans belief that planets orbited the Earth upon giant wheels, that the more complex the idea becomes with age, the more likely it is to be wrong. This situation occurs because if an idea is wrong, it constantly has to be amended and re-amended as new information is deduced or discovered.

Startled to be even considering the possibility that the idea of time might be a mistake, I began to wonder if anyone in his right mind had ever dared to challenge this most basic and fundamental of all-human beliefs? Is it insanity to think time doesn't exist?

But if time doesn't exist, what does? What were ancient peoples really observing, the effects of time, or the effects of motion? Although motion is associated with time, maybe this idea is wrong, maybe it is the other way around - *maybe it is time that is associated with motion*!

I was about to go on, but it was just too hot.

I overstayed my time limit in the pool, got overheated, and just barely made it up the ladder. I crawled out of the big hole, and half staggered into the welcomed shade of a Banyan tree. The alarmed homeowner, who witnessed my shaky efforts from his window, opened the door and came outside with a glass of water. He asked me if I was all right, and when I didn't answer immediately, he threw it right in my face; apologizing as he did it because he thought I was going to pass out. Which wasn't true at all, I was merely trying to re-focus my thinking onto the problem of time and didn't want to interrupt my train of thought by talking to him.

When he told me he was going down to the store to buy me some Gatorade, I mumbled to him to go. I was glad to see him go. I was glad he was getting out of the way, because after 15 years of aimless searching, I was finally getting someplace! After he left, I observed clouds coming towards me and knew they would bring a welcome drop in the temperature. Knowing that I could return to the pool later and do more work when it was cool, I returned to my thoughts; or rather to one single thought which was uppermost in my mind: if "time" was not creating the phenomenon of time, then what was?

It didn't take long to realize there was only one possibility - motion!

Of course! It was suddenly all so simple. What was early man really observing? Motion! Harmonic motion! And then the truth about the development of time was finally made clear. The development of the concept of time was a mistake. A mistaken attempt made by men ignorant of the motions of the Earth in their efforts to assign a cause to the celestial phenomenon they were witnessing!

I was thunderstruck! The problem with mans vision of the universe was "time"! Time itself! "Time" does not exist and never has! The great mistake in Einstein's vision of the universe was suddenly apparent. One of the five fundamental principles of the universe - matter, space, time, energy, and the forces of nature - didn't exist! And Albert Einstein, just like all of his predecessors, had also based his scientific vision of the universe upon something that doesn't exist!

How simple! How extraordinarily simple! I was flabbergasted!

This was one of the great days in my life. On that day, the world changed! Stars collided in space, universities toppled, and new ones sprouted up like magic in their place. The race was on again. The error in mankind's scientific vision of the universe was no longer a possibility, it was a reality! And I was excited!

The universe was constructed in a different manner to the way men believed. If I could find out how it was constructed, and if higher dimensional space was part of this new reality, it would prove that Jesus knew more about the construction of the universe than all of the greatest scientists who had ever lived! An incomparable discovery of unparalleled importance! A discovery unlike any other ever made in all of human history.

Thinking the above thoughts, I felt a deep sense of responsibility to everyone everywhere. I was in one of the most unique positions experienced by only a few people in all of human history: I and I alone possessed the knowledge that would change the lives and the destiny of every person in every country in the world. The knowledge that would directly affect the science, the technology and the religion of all future generations to come!

In honor of the position fate had bestowed upon me, I quit my job and went to work!

Ch9 THE CURIOUS RELATIONSHIP BETWEEN TIME AND MOTION

In the following months, I spent most of my evenings in the tall, stately library in downtown Fort Lauderdale. It was great to be searching for the truth again, and it felt even greater to have the zest for life return. A feeling I hadn't felt for years. But it had been a long time since I had done any kind of academic study, and I wondered if I was up to the challenge. However, I soon found that old habits die hard, and oddly enough, the construction of this magnificent library helped.

The Fort Lauderdale Library is much more than a library, it is a celebration of libraries. If architecture were music, this place would be a symphony.

I don't recall when I first walked into this library, but I do remember being surprised when I did. I was surprised because instead of seeing the many racks of books I expected to find – a huge gallery five stories high stood silently in front of me. Although there were elevators, one lone staircase somehow found its way up along the western side of this massive, and curious void. I use the words "curious void" because every time I climbed this stairway within this building of knowledge, I had the strange sensation that death stalked beside me!

I felt this sensation because the stairs were merely slats covered with carpet, and when I looked between them as I climbed upward [especially between the fifth and sixth floors], the lobby seemed dangerously far below. Fascinated by this sight, I realized I was merely stepping upon boards suspended high in the air, and when I did, I knew my mind was wandering and I must quickly re-focus my attention upon the next step. If not, I felt I might lose my perspective, lose my balance, and with just one slip, tumble over the low handrail and spiral to my death far below: a curious feeling within a building whose purpose is devoted to storing the knowledge of the human race!

Perhaps this feeling was intentionally created. Maybe the architect was trying to convey some emotion he was feeling. Perhaps he was trying to tell us all that the empty void represents death, while the knowledge we are climbing the stairs to obtain represents life. And if men do not continually focus their concentration upon the next step on the path of knowledge, they might stumble and suffer the ultimate penalty for it! But

49

then again, perhaps I was just daydreaming.

Then again, to dream dreams was why I was there: to dream the dreams no man had ever dreamed before; to think the thoughts no man had ever thought before; and to discover the secrets no man had ever discovered before.

And that is where it happened. In the quiet library standing in the center of the city that had once been the party capital of the United States, I discovered the mysteries of "time".

I would like to be able to say that everything happened dramatically, in one brilliant shining burst of inspiration, but it didn't. Instead it occurred slowly and patiently, as evening after evening I sat before a table upon the sixth floor and looked out through the giant glass windows at the city far below. Many times, I just sat there silently, watching the day end. Watching the shadows lengthening behind tall buildings and creeping up the sides of the ones behind them. Like a silent chorus of motion, millions of shadows all moving together in harmony. An army of effects, all moving in sync to one grand cause - the Sun. [An observation that was soon to have great significance!]

Within that library I was happy. The quiet intellectual atmosphere reminded me of college. I studied there and thought there. And it was there that I first began to realize there is an inextricable relationship between time and motion. An inextricable relationship that begins to become apparent the more one investigates the *measurement* of time.

For instance, I asked myself, is it just a coincidence that all measurements of time are defined by motion? The answer is no! Everything men can think of that might possibly be used to measure the passage of time is in motion. There is no exception. Even tree rings in dead logs were laid down by chemical reactions taking place at fixed rates.

Chemical reactions also play a major role in "Biological Time". The DNA in plants and animals responsible for the growth and characteristics of all living things are made of chemicals reacting with other chemicals.

Even when we think we are sitting perfectly still, there are billions of chemical reactions taking place within every cell of our body. Some people think they can detect a passage of time by sitting perfectly still in a dark room. But what these people fail to realize is that their body is a microcosm of activity. Their heart is beating. Blood is flowing to every cell throughout their body. Electricity is flowing from their nerves to their brains. Within the brain, neurons are constantly receiving and passing electric current, generating a succession of thoughts. Which all lead us to the realization that even though we are sitting still, our body, is a virtual metropolis of chemical and biological motions.

These chemical and biological motions create a sequence of events, which are responsible for our aging process. The chemistry of our DNA becomes a chemical "clock" that makes our body "tick". Knowing this we also know that our ages are not a result of time, but the result of chemical reactions.

The realization that no measurement of time is free of motion inspired my imagination. I tried to think of a way to philosophically prove the existence of this unbreakable bond between motion and time. As a result of these efforts, a fascinating philosophical conjecture was conceived. It started like this, "If all of the motions of everything in the universe slowed down, stopped and then slowly started up again, is there any way to tell for how long they were stopped?"

The answer, after much consideration, is no. Because just as a physical yardstick measures the distance between two objects, a regularly reoccurring sequence of events - harmonic motion - is used as a yardstick of time to measure the distance between a random set of events. However, unlike the physical yardstick, when the harmonic motion used to keep track of time stops, the yardstick of time no longer exists and the distance between random events can no longer be measured. Hence, we are unable to tell if the universe was stopped for a second, a day, a year, or a million years!

Also, in such a slowdown, since the motions of everything in the universe would slow down proportionally to the motions of everything else, we would never notice any change occurring at all. We would never notice anything slowing down, stopping, or starting up again. In fact, nothing would ever appear to have happened at all. A simply astounding conclusion!

Based on this conclusion, I began to understand that time is a function of motion, a phenomenon created by motion, and as such cannot exist separately and apart from motion. Just like the shadows I observed every evening while looking out of the window of the library were an effect, time is also an effect and motion is the cause. (Although later, I discovered that motion is not the final cause. Motion itself is an effect being created by still another cause. Time is merely the last effect in a chain of causes and effects. But all this will be explained later.)

After coming to the conclusion that time is a function of motion, a phenomenon created by motion, something else began to bother me. Each night when I was about to leave the library, I reluctantly looked at the clock to see what time it was. This nightly observation troubled me greatly. Like the rest of us, I had always associated time with clocks, and clocks with time. I was troubled to think that a clock, the most common of all mechanical devices, was keeping track of something that didn't exist.

Or rather, I should say I was troubled until I realized that even though time does not exist, the phenomenon of time does. The phenomenon of time is real. Just like the shadows creeping up the sides of the buildings surrounding the library is a real phenomenon, and just like the motion of the stars circling the Earth is a real phenomenon, the phenomenon of time is also a real phenomenon. It exists as a "real illusion".

Since I was excited about what I had discovered, I made the mistake of telling a friend that time exists only as a phenomenon, and not as a fundamental principle of the universe. For my efforts, I was rudely shown a clock and asked, "If time doesn't exist, what the hell is that keeping track of?"

Because of that little incident, I realized I was playing with fire. I understood that anytime you attack a belief, you are instigating an irrational emotional response. Therefore, I decided that from then on, I would go within, and tell no one what I was doing. But just in case I was ever confronted with the same response again, I researched clocks.

This research revealed that the great fallacy of clocks keeping track of "time" is dispelled when one investigates the role of the clock as a navigational device.

In reality, a clock is a mechanical device keeping track of a fixed position upon the surface of the rotating Earth relative to the fixed position of the Sun when it is directly overhead. The hour, the minute, and the second were arbitrary units assigned to time long ago and are meaningless. Over the years, time has merely become associated with clocks and clocks with time.

When someone asks another, "What time is it?" in reality and unbeknownst to themselves, what they are really asking is, "According to the clock - how far has the Earth rotated since the Sun was directly overhead at noon?" Since the circumference of the Earth at the equator is divided into twenty four sections, each about a thousand miles in width, and the clock is divided into twenty four hours, every hour past noon indicates the Earth has rotated a little over a thousand miles. The further breakdown of the clock into minutes and seconds allows this thousand-mile distance to be divided into thirty-six hundred equal parts, which allows the navigator to accurately determine his position to about a quarter of a mile.

This relationship between the Earthly location of a clock and the position of the Sun is made apparent by airplane travel. When we travel from America to Europe, we have to change our clocks when we arrive, if not, they will be out of sync with the position of the Sun and their "time" is inaccurate.

The arbitrariness of our increments of time - the hour, minute, second, day, week, month, and year is exposed when considering the rotation of other planets. When men go to Mars, all of these units will have to be changed. Since Mars rotates approximately one half hour longer (24.5 hours) than the Earth's 24 hours, an Earthly clock taken to Mars will soon be out of sync with the appearance of the Sun in the Martian sky. After 12 "Martian days", an Earthly clock taken to Mars will be 6 hours slow. And after 24 Martian days, it will be 12 hours slow. The discrepancy will really become apparent then, because even though the Earthly clock indicates it is midnight, the Sun will be shining high in the sky, showing everyone it is noon!

If a man upon the surface of Mars tries to navigate using Earthly clocks, he will get lost. He will find that the Earthly clock is useless upon Mars. To be able to navigate upon Mars, men will have to build completely new clocks that correspond to the slower rotation of the Martian world.

When he builds new clocks, he will find that he will have to change the length of the hour, minute, and second to correspond to the longer rotational period of the Martian planet.

If he stays for generations, the earthy concept of the hour, minute, and second will become meaningless. He may eventually find it necessary to substitute the values of the Earthly second with the values of the slower Martian second. A substitution which will affect his values for all the important measurements which are based upon the value of an Earthly second (such as the speed of light). Hence, all of his mathematical equations for objects in motion will also be affected. He will then find it necessary to have two sets of reference books: one for values based upon the measurement of an Earthly second, and one for the Martian second.

Or he may find it necessary to do away with the concept of the hour, minute and second altogether. He may find it more efficient to divide a Martian day into a "metric system" of units, such as tenths, hundredths, and thousandths.

Although this is all speculation, it is a good illustration to demonstrate that our concept of hours, minutes and seconds, are ONLY meaningful upon this planet or upon another planet rotating once every 24 "Earthly hours". When we try to use our clocks upon another planet rotating at a different rate of speed, we find that our "earthly clocks" are unsuited for the task. This failure unmasks the truth about the units of time and we finally begin to realize that our concept of the hour, minute, and second is not universal. We begin to realize clocks do not keep track of "time". "Time" is merely associated with clocks, and clocks are merely associated with time.

After writing down these thoughts upon the fallacy of clocks, I decided it was "time" to leave the realm of philosophy and discover a way to prove everything I was thinking. And, lo and behold! After a long search, I rediscovered the Michelson Morley Experiment. [The subject of one of the last lectures I had listened to before quitting school so many years ago!]

Ch10 THE MICHELSON MORLEY EXPERIMENT

At the beginning of this book I made the statement that it seemed as if some of the major events in my life were meant to happen to compel me to go search for the ultimate mysteries of the universe. And now, while thinking about the Michelson Morley Experiment, it made me realize that it was almost as if another impulsive action of mine – that took place years before - was meant to happen to keep me from being misinformed!

Years earlier, when I quit school, I thought my rash act was purely impulsive. I was in Third Semester Physics, and had just finished studying the Michelson Morley Experiment when I got up and walked out of class. But if I had not walked out at that particular point in the curriculum of that particular course, I never would have been able to discover the error in Einstein's vision of the universe.

Like everybody else who studied Physics, eventually, I probably would have been indoctrinated into believing Einstein's ideas about the fourth dimension of time. Faced with the *supposedly* overwhelming evidence, and the never-ending insistence of today's teachers that Relativity is the truth, the whole truth, and nothing but the truth, it is possible that I would have ended up believing that his vision of time was correct. I would never even have thought of questioning the idea of time. Who knows, I might even have accepted the popular belief that anyone who thinks there is something wrong with the Theory of Relativity is either uneducated, or a fool.

Perhaps I might have fallen into the trap that traps so many: human arrogance. I might have believed that since I had worked so hard to understand the workings of the most difficult theory in all of science, I was to be congratulated, that perhaps there is nothing wrong with it after all. I might have even tried to incorporate it into the vision of the universe I was trying to deduce, and in the end, would have ended up no better off than any of the physicists who dogmatically teach this theory as doctrine.

Luckily that was not the case.

Although I ardently admired Einstein, I never became a believer. A common trait I unknowingly held with a man recognized as the greatest scientist of his era: Albert Michelson.

Michelson was a physicist who became famous for creating what has come to be known as the "Michelson Morley Experiment": one of the most important experiments ever conducted in science.

Tragically, this was an experiment most of the people of the world have never heard about. Which is a shame, considering that the explanation of this one scientific experiment alone forces us to define precisely how matter, space, and time are constructed – definitions which are then used to explain how the entire physical universe is constructed. Explanations which both directly and indirectly affect the lives of every person upon this planet!

Although it is hard to believe, the explanation of this one relatively unknown experiment was instrumental in creating mankind's present vision of matter, space, and time. Since the physicists of the Twentieth Century also considered this experiment to be a proof of Einstein's Theory of Relativity (never mind that Michelson rejected Einstein's explanation) a little background information on both how and why it was conducted is essential.

It all began towards the end of the last century, when two prominent American physicists, Albert Michelson, a Nobel Prize winner, and Edward Morley, his colleague, devised an experiment using mirrors and light to detect the presence of the "Aether wind".

Just as a ship moving through the ocean creates a wake, the scientists of that era believed the earth created a similar wake or a "wind" as it moved through the "Aether" - the name given to the substance they thought space was made of.

To detect the presence of the "Aether wind," Michelson and Morley first built a relatively simple apparatus. This consisted of two sets of mirrors set at equal lengths, and arranged perpendicular to each other. Between them was a lightly silvered mirror that allowed the light beams to penetrate through it as well as be reflected off of it. The basic idea was to turn on a light source, allow a beam of light to first shine on the silvered mirror where it then split - reflected off both sets of the other mirrors, and was then reassembled at a target.

Because the earth is orbiting the sun at an average speed of approximately sixty-six thousand miles an hour, when mirrors three and four (see FIGURE 10-1) were parallel to the Earth's direction of motion and one and two were perpendicular to it, the mathematics indicated that the travel times between mirrors one and two should be shorter than the travel times between mirrors three and four. And the interference pattern created by the different arrival times of these two beams of light at the target should indicate this result, but it was never seen! To Michelson and Morley's surprise, the pattern they saw at the target indicated that there was no difference in the travel times whatsoever!

[To simplify the principles involved, the following <u>abbreviated diagram</u> of Michelson and Morley's apparatus is placed against the backdrop of the Earth.]
FIGURE 10-1

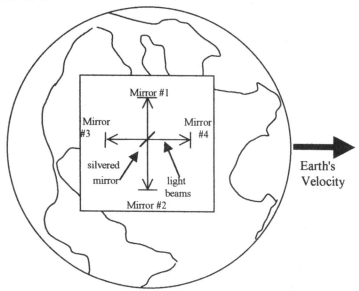

Although surprised, Michelson and Morley were undaunted. They simply built a better apparatus and tried the experiment all over again. But just as before, they still came up with the same results.

Although other people might have quit, Michelson and Morley didn't! They improved the apparatus and tried again; and again and again, but to no avail. The pattern on the screen continued to show that the two beams were always traveling at the same speed.

But Michelson and Morley were true believers; they never gave up. They tried for twenty years! They improved their apparatus until it was so sensitive to vibration, it had to be placed upon a two ton slab of sandstone floating in a pool of mercury because an ox pulling a cart down a road close to their building would interfere with it. But even that didn't change the results!

No matter how long they tried, and no matter how sensitive they made their apparatus, the results were always the same - the differences between the travel times they expected to see were not seen. There was no difference between the two travel times whatsoever!

Enter George Fitzgeralds and Hendrik Lorentz.

Fitzgeralds an Irish physicist, and Lorentz a German physicist, both working independently of each other, thought of a way that would make both of these travel times equal. Each one of them proposed that if the Aether wind compressed the matter of the earth in the direction of travel by "just the right amount", the distance between mirrors #3 and #4 would shorten. This shorter distance would then shorten the travel time of the light beam moving between these two mirrors, making its travel time equal to the travel time of the beam moving between mirrors #1 and #2. Figure 10-2

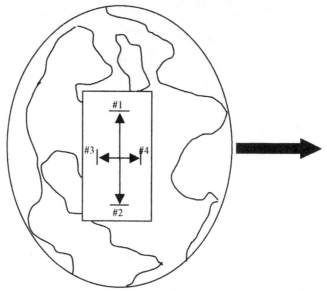

Also, since the Earth speeds up slightly and slows down slightly during the different seasons as it orbits the Sun - although these changes are incredibly minute - because Michelson and Morley's apparatus was now so super sensitive, this change should have been seen too. But it wasn't.

Because it wasn't seen, Lorentz further suggested that if time "itself" somehow slowed down by "just the right amount" no change would ever be noticed. However, the seemingly improbable idea that the Aether wind somehow compressed matter "just enough" to fool the instruments was seen by other physicists as an "ad hoc" solution to the problem and was dismissed as being too contrived.

Since no other explanations were available, no other explanations were presented. And the world of physics had to wait for a solution.

But they didn't have to wait long. When Albert Einstein's ideas began to influence the world of physics, the solution to the problem seemed apparent. According to Einstein's vision of the universe matter was made of something, space was made on nothing, and time was relative and existed as a fourth dimension of the universe he called "space-time." This meant that there was no Aether and no Aether wind. This also meant that the measurement of time was relative to the speed of the observer. And when these ideas were combined with his brilliant deduction that the measurement of the speed of light was the same for all observers, scientists finally believed they had finally found the explanation for the Michelson Morley experiment.

However, even though Einstein's vision of matter, space, and time has been extremely successful in some areas, it has utterly failed in others. The most important of these failures is its inability to unite the four forces of nature into one "grand unification theory", or adequately explain why they cannot be united: a seemingly trivial technical observation that acquires a status of great philosophical importance. Even those who are uninitiated into the workings of science can easily understand that the true vision of the universe must be able to explain not just some of the phenomenon of nature, *but all of it! Every last bit of it!*

A deduction Einstein himself must have been acutely aware of because he spent most of the remaining years of his life trying to unite the forces of nature into his own personal vision of matter, space, and time. Sadly failing in the attempt because there was no chance of succeeding! No chance of succeeding because Einstein's failure was not due to a lack of ability or effort, but rather due to his erroneous vision of one of the basic building blocks with which he used to construct *his* vision of the universe – "time!"

Because if time is not a fundamental principle of the universe; if time is a function of motion and cannot exist apart from motion, then time is NOT a building block of the universe, and cannot be used as one. If time is a function of motion, it is a phenomenon created by motion. Hence, it cannot be used as the fundamental cause to explain time dilation. If it cannot, then the length shrinkage and time dilation effects proposed by Lorentz in response to the results of the Michelson Morley Experiment, *are being created by the increased velocity of the atoms themselves as they move through space!*

Consequently, there must exist a hidden, intrinsic relationship between matter, space, and velocity that nobody previously suspected. A secret relationship which unites rather than separates these three seemingly different aspects of the universe's construction! A relationship whose interactions create an exact mechanical and mathematical explanation for the results of the Michelson Morley Experiment - a relationship that reveals the *True Vision of the Universe*!

I was excited. Although science presently believes the true vision of the universe was discovered when Einstein introduced the Theory of Relativity, I now knew this was wrong.

The true vision of the universe had not been discovered at all! It was still there, waiting to be found! A sight no man has ever seen before!

Suddenly, I felt like an explorer of old. An adventurer who hears a legend about a lost continent at the end of the world; who gets a ship and sails towards the horizon in search of whatever awaits him.

But this time, it would be no ordinary quest. This would be the ultimate quest for the ultimate prize! The ultimate search for the ultimate vision of everything! And like the view of the Grand Canyon, or Niagara Falls, the ultimate vision of the universe must be an awesome spectacle to behold.

But to be able to be the first man to ever see this true vision of the universe, I realized I and I alone would have to first discover the secret of how matter, space and velocity are related.

Why me? There was no one else! Those who can discover it won't, and the rest never will.

Those scientists who are capable of discovering the answer are unwilling to challenge the Theory of Relativity. They are either true believers in Relativity, and don't think there is anything wrong with it, or they are afraid of the loss of their credibility if they make any controversial statements to their colleagues. So it is sad to realize that those who can discover the truth about the universe - won't!

Unfortunately, the rest of the people in the world will never discover the truth either. They do not have the powerful motivation, the "time", or the desperate need to discover the answer to this problem. Therefore, I knew it was up to me.

To me! Suddenly, I felt alone. Who in the hell was I? I was not a physicist.

Feeling inept, I desperately wanted an ally, a seeker like myself. Someone who passionately sought the truth and would go anywhere and do anything necessary to discover it! But I knew no help would be forthcoming. I was alone. It was a hard truth to accept, but after I had reluctantly accepted it, what the hell!

I had started alone, and I must now finish alone. I had come much further than I had ever expected. A little bit further wouldn't hurt. The hardest part of any journey is the last part. So I prepared myself for the finale.

I bought books on math and physics. I reviewed calculus. I went to the library and studied the latest discoveries in science. To increase my self-confidence I lifted weights in the evening, and did push ups and sit-ups in the morning. I didn't crawl out of bed; I leaped out of bed. I fasted, lost weight, and felt good. To be a winner, you must first feel like a winner. To succeed, you must already be a success.

And I was successful beyond my wildest dreams!

I took a mental journey through the innermost foundations of the physical universe. I saw what no man has ever seen before, and I discovered the answers to the greatest mysteries of both science and religion!

Ch11 BENT SPACE?

Years before, when I was in school, I reduced everything in the physical universe down to its five most basic parts: matter, space, time, energy, and the forces of nature. Next, I tried to define how each piece was constructed, and then I looked at the individual parts searching for some sort of error I knew must exist. But I failed to find it.

I failed to find it because I did not know where to look, or what to look for. But not anymore, now I was ready!

Space was where the problem was. I knew this to be true because if time does not exist as a fundamental principle of the universe, then the fourth dimension made of "space-time" does not exist either.

This error can only mean one thing, that just like the mistakes of our ancient ancestors, 20th Century science has also based its vision of the universe upon the effects it sees instead of the cause of those effects. The explanation of space is based upon what appears to be there instead of what is really there.

So how can this disparity be resolved? How can the true vision of space reveal itself?

The answer is easy. The true vision of the universe might be revealed if some characteristic of space is found that can be used to change our perspective and see space from its point of view instead of from our point of view.

But what can we find? Where can we look?

There is only one place to look - amidst the current beliefs of space.

What are these beliefs?

According to the present scientific model of the universe given to us by Albert Einstein, space is "believed" to be made of nothing. But even though it is made of nothing, it is somehow "believed" to be constructed out of three observable dimensions of length, width, and height, and one dimension of time. (This doesn't seem to make any sense, because how can something made of nothing have any characteristics at all?)

Furthermore, Einstein also proposed that space appeared to be bent around massive objects such as stars, and that bent space is equivalent to the force of gravity! (However, as was said before, how can something made of nothing be bent?)

Although this idea doesn't seem to trouble scientists, it troubled me; because how can those who claim to believe only in those things perceptible to the human senses, turn right around and profess to believe in the "bend-ability" of a substance made of nothing at all? Such logic makes no sense. The only idea that made any sense was for space to indeed be made of something.

Therefore, temporarily accepting this premise, I proceeded along this line of reasoning to see where it would lead me; and lo and behold, I found that the bend-ability of space, combined with a 20th Century discovery made by Astronomers, is the first key to understanding how space is really constructed.

After studying Astronomy, I realized the bend-ability of space does indeed appear to be a real phenomenon. Space appears to be bent around massive objects like stars. During solar eclipses, the sky closest to the Sun was dark enough for astronomers to see the stars that the bright light from the Sun usually obscured. When pictures were taken of these stars, and compared to other pictures taken at night of this same region of the sky, the stars in the pictures taken during the eclipse appeared to have changed position slightly. An effect that indicated the space close to the Sun was bending the path of the light passing through it. An observation that seemed to indicate the space closest to the Sun must somehow be bent.

Accepting this conclusion as a real observation, a real effect, I decided to investigate its cause.

While thinking about it, I realized my first job was to determine if this bend was inward or outward. Using the force of gravity, this problem was easily solved: since the force of gravity pulls objects towards the Sun, I hypothesized that space was bent *inwards* towards the Sun rather than away from it.

Next, because this inward bend was creating real effects, it was only logical to surmise that it must be created by something that was real too. So what was it?

Even though stars are enormous beyond the ability to describe, I knew that a star is nothing more than a massive collection of individual particles. So if space was indeed bent around a star, the bend in space had to be a result of all of the individual bends surrounding all the individual particles of which the star was constructed. Since a star is constructed out of atoms, and atoms are constructed out of a nucleus of protons and neutrons surrounded by a swarm of electrons, these particles had to be responsible for generating the bent space surrounding the star.

In other words, the summation of all the bent spaces surrounding all of the particles in a star was somehow creating one large massive bend in space. But which particles were responsible for the bend? To assume they were all responsible might be a wrong assumption.

In order to solve this dilemma, I took another look at Isaac Newton's law of gravity, noting that the force of gravity is directly proportional to the amount of mass present. I reasoned that since the majority of the mass of the atom is contained within the protons and neutrons [which are approximately eighteen hundred times more massive than an electron], the majority of the mass of a star must consist mainly of protons and neutrons.

Consequently, I concluded that the majority of the bent space surrounding a star had to be the result of the summation of all the individual bent spaces surrounding protons and neutrons (the electron will be discussed later). Therefore, the bend in space surrounding a star somehow had to be a direct result of the individual characteristics of the protons and neutrons themselves. In other words, protons and neutrons had to be generating the force of gravity!

Although this deduction seemed elementary, try as I might, I could not yet figure how these particles were generating a force! However, the more I thought about the bend-ability of space, the more I began to realize that space must be elastic, and if it was elastic, it had to possess the ability to stretch!

Stretch? Of course! Why hadn't I thought of it before!

Ch12 "LESS DENSE", AND FLOWING SPACE!

The ability of anything to stretch is very important.

When something stretches, its density changes. This fact leads to some startling possibilities about space!

If space was indeed bent inward around the Sun, space would be stretched. This stretched space would be less dense nearer to the Sun than further away. Since the Sun is a sphere, a large spherical region of less dense space would surround it, like a pea surrounded by a basketball.

This would mean that the bent space theorized to surround planets and stars is only an effect being created by something else. It is a phenomenon being generated by less dense space. Space only appears to be bent because the Sun is a sphere.

This deduction is important because it indicates that the force of gravity would *not* be the result of "bent space", as Einstein believed - *but rather, the result of less dense space!* And this deduction leads to an even more startling conclusion for the individual particles the sun is made of!

When the Sun moves through space, the space directly ahead, in the pathway of the Sun, is continually being bent inward towards the Sun as it approaches, then back outwards to its original position as the Sun passes by. Consequently, since stars are mainly composed of protons and neutrons, the same phenomenon would also occur as they too move through space. Making it logical to conclude that space itself ebbs and flows in wave like patterns as matter passes through it.

This conclusion made me realize that if the four forces of nature are in some way related to each other, then they are all effects being created by the same cause. Therefore, if gravity is the result *of less denser space*, it was possible that the other three forces of nature might also be manifestations of space! If space possesses an elasticity that allows it to bend - giving it the ability to move, maybe it can flow too!

If this is indeed so, the electrostatic charges of electrons and protons could be the result of flowing space! Just as less dense space could be responsible for the force of gravity, flowing space might be responsible for the creation of the electromagnetic force! (Remember the THIRD GREAT CLUE from Chapter 6?)

This was an exciting idea, and a fascinating vision to behold. Just imagine, currents of space flowing like miniature rivers through the universe. It was a delightful thought. Was I the first person to ever conceive it? Amidst the billions of people thinking trillions of thoughts, was this thought never thought of before? I knew instinctively it was worthy of closer inspection; but little did I know then that this intriguing idea was but the key to deducing the fantastic truth about the particles we call electrons, protons, and neutrons. (They are not particles at all!)

As explained in Chapter 6, the Electromagnetic force is the name given to the positive and negative "poles" associated with magnets, and the positive and negative "charges" on tiny particles such as electrons and protons. This Electromagnetic force is divided into two forces: the magnetic force, and the electrostatic force.

The magnetic force is mainly identified by the *lines* of "flux" which are seen surrounding magnets (FIGURE 6-7); while the electrostatic force is associated with *lines* pointing directly towards or away from particles like the proton and the electron (FIGURE 6-6). *Lines* which might really represent "currents" of three dimensional space flowing around magnets, and into and out of protons and electrons!

Now if this vision is real, if these currents really do exist, and if the electromagnetic force is the result of flowing space, there has to be a reason why three-dimensional space is flowing. Also, because there is a positive and negative charge, there have to be two directions to the flow. With one flow moving towards a particle of one charge (such as the proton), while the other flow moves away from a particle of the opposite charge (such as the electron).

Combining these two ideas, I concluded that since the electrostatic charges point directly at protons and electrons from all three directions at once, then three-dimensional space must be flowing directly into one particle and directly out of the other. (Remember the SECOND GREAT CLUE from Chapter 6?)

But where! Where is three-dimensional space flowing to, and where is it coming from?

There was only one answer: higher dimensional space! Of course! It was suddenly all so simple.

Higher dimensional space would be the exact location for three-dimensional space to flow into and out of. In other words, three-dimensional space must be flowing directly into one particle, and then out of this particle into higher dimensional space. While from the other particle, the three-dimensional space is returning from its trip into higher dimensional space, and flowing back into the three-dimensional space it originally came from.

Suddenly, I sat back in my chair stunned! Was it possible?

Yes it was! If the above reasoning is true, it leads to a simply astounding conclusion - that protons and electrons are not *particles* at all!

PROTONS AND ELECTRONS ARE THREE-DIMENSIONAL HOLES IN SPACE!!!

Ch13 PROTONS AND ELECTRONS ARE HOLES IN SPACE!

Three-dimensional holes! What an incredible vision!

Just imagine all of the matter in the universe being made of nothing at all! Never, even in our wildest dreams would anybody ever think that matter is made of nothing. Like "time", it is one of only a mere handful of beliefs about the universe that none of us would ever even consider challenging.

Our concept of matter is very important to our mental well being too. Matter not only gives us physical support; it also gives us a certain amount of mental support as well. Without ever thinking about it, we feel secure as we stand upon it, sit upon it, and sleep upon it. If you have ever been upon a ship in a rolling sea, you understand the statement; "It is good to be back on solid ground again."

The idea that matter is made of something is perhaps the most unquestionable question there is. Next to the concept of time, it is perhaps the single most commonly shared belief amongst all of the people upon this planet; and to suddenly throw it away temporarily knocks us off our psychological center of gravity.

If you haven't yet felt the full impact of this disturbing idea, look at your body. Its "solidness" is an illusion. It is really a massive collection of microscopic holes. It is shocking to contemplate, but we are made of nothing at all!

I have mentioned these uncomfortable feelings because the deep contemplation of this revelation created a psychological uneasiness within me that was only comforted by my religious beliefs. I found solace from the awful thought that the physical body is a void, in the soothing and comforting belief that we also possess an immortal soul – that God himself created. A second, unseen part of ourselves that exists in higher dimensional space!

Feeling a little better, I pressed on, but not without mixed emotions. Although I was intellectually thrilled, I needed to know if three-dimensional holes could actually exist. Was there any precedent upon which to justify this truly extraordinary and revolutionary conclusion?

The answer was yes.

From my previous studies of space and its dimensions, I realized that in three-dimensional space, there could only be two-dimensional holes. All pipe ends, doors, windows, cave openings, etc are two-dimensional holes. Furthermore, the tops and bottoms of tornadoes, hurricanes and whirlpools are two-dimensional openings allowing passage into the third dimension.

The mental picture of these two-dimensional openings allowing passage into the third dimension is the analogy that allows us to realize all holes are one dimension smaller than the number of dimensions that are present.

This relationship occurs because each surface is one dimension smaller that the volume it envelops. For example, the surface of a three-dimensional volume is two-dimensional, while the surface of a fourth-dimensional volume is three-dimensional. With these ideas in mind, it is easy to see that to enter into the interior of a volume, its surface must first be penetrated. Because the surface is always one dimension smaller than the volume, the hole is always one dimension smaller than the volume it enters.

Therefore, if fourth-dimensional space does indeed exist, even though it cannot be seen, one characteristic indicative of its presence will be the existence of three-dimensional holes. Just like two-dimensional holes allow passage into the third dimension, three-dimensional spherical shaped holes allow passage into the fourth dimension.

If fifth-dimensional space exists, there will be additional fourth-dimensional holes* within these three-dimensional holes, and so on and so forth depending upon how many dimensions exist, and how many dimensions are penetrated.

The incredible vision of space flowing into and out of these three-dimensional holes cemented my belief that space had to be made of something. For if the electron and the proton are indeed three-dimensional holes in space, and if space is supposedly made of nothing, then how could nothing flow into nothing?

The only logical answer was that space could not be made of "nothing". Space had to be made of something! Nor is this idea a return to the old Aether Theory.

In the Aether Theory, it was believed that space was made of something, and that matter was made of solids. This relationship was similar to the way in which ice floats in the ocean (which is probably where the idea originated). The vision that matter was made of something and space was made of something caused men to believe that

---

* An idea that suddenly sounds like an excellent explanation for Quarks.

the earth displaced the Aether and created a "wind" as it moved through it – in the same way that a wake is created in front of a boat. A wind the Michelson Morley Experiment proved did not exist.

In contrast to the old Aether Theory, this analysis was slowly revealing that contrary to present belief, it was *space that was made of something and matter that was made of nothing*!

Space could now be viewed as a multidimensional substance whose three-dimensional surface (our three-dimensional universe), is inundated with a myriad of three-dimensional holes: kind of like Swiss Cheese. Furthermore, there is no "Aether Wind" because matter does not displace space as it moves. When matter is constructed out of holes, space is not "blown" to either side as matter passes by. Instead, space reconfigures itself around these three-dimensional holes as they move.

Although it might sound kind of hackneyed to use the analogy of the holes in Swiss cheese, this concept helps envision the relationship between matter and space. The perspective is just reversed. For example, in Swiss cheese, we see the cheese but not the holes, while in the universe, we see the holes but not the cheese. Spherical holes!

It is fascinating to know that if you can see the holes but not the space, these holes will look like tiny spheres - exactly how present day science sees protons and electrons! (Remember the FIRST GREAT CLUE from Chapter 6?)

Philosophizing upon this new relationship between matter and space made me think of the great poetic pathway to God enlightenment in Hinduism: the Jnana Yoga, the pathway of knowledge. However, instead of saying, "I am that, Thou art that, That is that", perhaps it should be said, "I am not that, Thou art not that, and that is not that!" because: *"Everything is nothing, and nothing is everything!"*

Although this is a play on words, - it is also a good description of the universe. All of my life, like everyone else, I just naturally assumed I was looking at the picture upon the photograph. Instead, I now realized I was really seeing the reverse image - the negative! It was hard to believe, but everything is opposite to what it appears to be. That which is made of something is not seen, and that which is made of nothing is seen!

And as I continued to toy with these ideas, I finally broke through the mental barrier between the 20th Century vision of the universe and the true vision! And when I did, almost instantly I achieved my first triumphant success! I discovered the answer to one of the great scientific mysteries of the universe. It happened like this...

Ch14 I MAKE THE FIRST GREAT BREAKTHROUGH

Because I did not know what was about to occur, I was continuing on - contemplating the ramifications of particles really being holes in three-dimensional space:

I was asking myself what seemed to be just a simple question, "...if three-dimensional space is flowing into one hole and out of the other, which one does it flow into, and which one does it flow out of?

Without knowing what I was about to discover, I reasoned that the solution to this problem might be found in the density of the space surrounding a hole. If three-dimensional space were flowing out of a hole, it was only logical to conclude that the density of the three-dimensional space immediately surrounding the hole would be greater than the density of the three-dimensional space further away. This effect would occur because the three-dimensional space flowing out of a hole pushes against the three-dimensional space already there, creating a spherical region of greater density, decreasing further away from the hole.

FIGURE 14-1

If the density of space were measured in *lines per inch*, the normal density of space might look something like this:

| | | | | | | | | | | | | | | | | | | | | | | | | | | | | | | | | | | | | |

But when space flows out of a hole, the density of the space immediately surrounding the hole changes. As indicated by the arrows, the surrounding space is *pushed* away from the hole. Note how a gradient forms around the hole with space being denser closer to the hole and less dense further away.

The opposite would be true for space flowing into a hole. If space were flowing into a hole, the space in the region directly surrounding it would be "pulled" - stretched into the hole. This pull would create a spherical region of less dense space immediately surrounding the hole; a region that slowly begins to return to its normal density much further away from the hole.

FIGURE 14-2

Density of space surrounding a hole that *space flows into*:
As indicated by the arrows, the surrounding space is *pulled* into this hole. Note too how the gradient formed here is less dense closer to the hole and denser further away.

When I considered which bend would be the best candidate for creating the source of gravity, I realized it had to be the bend surrounded by the less dense region of space. Within this less dense region, space would be "stretched inward". This less dense region would make the space surrounding other holes stretch towards it: making the hole move in that direction too.

Therefore, since I had previously concluded that protons and neutrons were responsible for creating the less dense space surrounding stars, it was only logical to conclude that three-dimensional space was flowing into the proton, and out of the electron.

Even though this idea was contrary to the present scientific beliefs of how the lines of electrostatic forces are pointing, I already knew that the direction of the positive and negative electrostatic forces were originally and arbitrarily assigned by Benjamin Franklin. Nobody knows for sure just which direction is which. [It should also be noted, that the mathematical proof of this theory, presented in the APPENDIX of this book, will work no matter what direction space flows.]

Wait a minute! What the hell!

Suddenly, I didn't care about "which direction was which." I didn't care about anything. Nothing mattered except for...Yes!!! There it was, right in front of me, the explanation for one of the greatest mysteries in all of science - the particle and wave characteristics of matter! It was unbelievable!

What was once perceived to be a very complicated idea was now rendered amazingly simple. The long trail of thought which led me to deduce the existence of less dense regions of space surrounding the proton and the electron now explained something totally unexpected!

Although many people nowadays understand that photons of energy possess both particle and wave characteristics, not many people are aware of the fact that matter does too. It seems to defy logic that matter should behave as both a particle and a wave, and yet it does. As strange as it seems, matter possesses characteristics which makes it behave both like a rock held in the hand, and sometimes like the waves it creates upon the surface of a pond after it is thrown in.

In the past there was no explanation for this dual phenomenon, but now there is: while the "holes" in three dimensional space are responsible for the particle effects of matter, the less dense (or denser) regions of space surrounding them are responsible for the "wave" effects of matter. Clearing up one of the great mysteries of science!

FIGURE 14-3

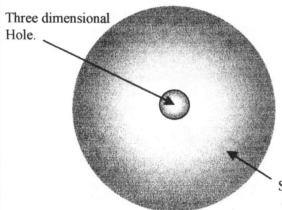

Three dimensional Hole.

Spherical region of dense or less dense space surrounding the hole.

Note, these proportions are not correct. The size of the spherical region of bent space surrounding individual particles appears to be immense. If the hole were the size of a bowling ball, the region of less dense space probably extends outward at least ten miles!

Ch15 I DISCOVER HOW ATOMS ARE REALLY CONSTRUCTED!

I couldn't believe it! Through the conscious use of this new way of thought, intentionally, I had unintentionally stumbled upon the answer to one of the great mysteries of science.

The paradox of the particle and wave characteristics of matter has long been one of the most perplexing phenomena in the whole of physics. Many experiments have been performed to try to understand it; millions have been spent in research; and the scientific discussions on this one subject alone could fill many volumes. And yet, with this new way of thinking and reasoning, the explanation of the particle and wave characteristics of matter was simple, almost trivial.

This was exciting. Finally, at long last, I was on to something! Something big!

Many years before I had reduced everything in the universe down to five separate parts: matter, space, time, energy, and the forces of nature. But now with a new way of thinking and reasoning, I had accomplished something that should be impossible! I had *united* two of these seemingly independent pieces - matter and space!

The implications of this discovery were shocking! Could all of the independent pieces of the universe actually be made out of only one thing! [One substance!]

The only way to find out was to try to unite another piece. But what piece? What could I try next?

I decided to try energy. But while thinking about it, I unexpectedly made another great discovery!

I started by thinking about atomic explosions. I knew atomic explosions are supposed to be the proof that matter and energy are equivalent (energy can be created out of the destruction of matter). Consequently, if matter was created out of bent and flowing space, maybe energy was too? But how? How was a hole in space and energy related?

I set out to find the answer by first trying to envision what was happening to the three-dimensional space flowing into the hole called the proton and out of the hole called the electron. What happens to this space? What happens to it after it flows into the proton, and before it flows out of the electron?

Although each question just seemed to raise another, the next question was actually the answer to all of them: since protons and electrons are in close proximity to each other in atoms, could the space flowing into one be flowing out of the other?

And then it came to me - vortices! Of course! Miniature tornadoes of three-dimensional space flowing from protons to electrons in higher dimensional space!

FIGURE 15-1

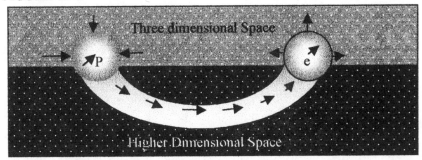

What a beautiful vision: an unimaginably small tornado of three-dimensional space flowing between particles in higher dimensional space! [As will be seen in the second book of this three-part trilogy, this most important discovery explains many of the totally bizarre and unexpected phenomenon of the sub-atomic world.]

Suddenly I stopped thinking about energy, when stunned, I realized this wonderful discovery suddenly explains the creation of atoms themselves!

Because three-dimensional space is flowing into the proton and out of the electron, when these two "particles" come into close proximity, a unique situation develops.

Although present day science says that the electrostatic charges of protons and electrons pull these two particles together, this is an oversimplification. What really happens is that some of the space flowing out of the electron begins to flow into the proton. As these two particles move closer together, a critical distance is reached where all of the three-dimensional space flowing out of the electron flows directly into the proton. When this situation occurs, *two* vortices of whirling space are created.

The first vortex is created in our three-dimensional space. (It flows from the electron to the proton.) The second vortex is in higher dimensional space. (This one flows from the proton to the electron in the opposite direction to the one flowing in three-dimensional space.)*

These two vortices now create a circulating flow containing a fixed volume of space.

This circulating volume of three-dimensional space flows from the proton, into higher dimensional space - through higher dimensional space, and then back into the electron. Here, it exits the electron, flowing back through three-dimensional space and into the proton once again- binding the proton to the electron, creating a hydrogen atom.

FIGURE 15-2

Three
Dimensional
Space

Higher
Dimensional
Space

When the circulating flow commences, both of the electrostatic charges are neutralized. The word "neutralized" was used because no flowing space escapes from the system. If surrounding space still flowed into or out of this system, atoms would possess electrical charges (and every time we touched something we would get shocked).

Because these vortices exist in all atoms throughout the universe, the revolutionary new vision of matter presented within this book was christened *The Vortex Theory*.

This knowledge of the internal structure of the hydrogen atom has an added bonus - incredibly, it finally allows us to understand how a photon of light is constructed!

*Note, the way a proton captures an electron not connected to it and forms a hydrogen atom will be explained in Book II of this three part trilogy.

Ch16 ENERGY IS FINALLY EXPLAINED TOO!

We all know that everywhere we look in nature we see an incredible variety of colors and shapes. However, what most of us don't know is that we never see anything! We don't even see the words on this page!

The only things we ever "see" are "photons" of energy.

Photons of energy are emitted from an energy source (such as the Sun, or a light bulb), hit the page, "bounce off", and hit our eyes. Without these photons we wouldn't be able to see anything at all. But just what are we "seeing"? What are these "photons" of energy? (What is energy?)

One of the greatest mysteries in all of physics is energy: just what is it?

According to present day science, energy is contained within tiny particles called photons. These photons possess both particle and wave characteristics. But where they come from, what they are made of, or how they are constructed is unknown.

But not anymore!

With the discovery of the miniature vortices flowing back and forth between protons and electrons, the great mystery of the photon is finally unraveled - and a fascinating vision unfolds before us.

What contemporary science calls a photon is really a condensed portion of three-dimensional space that is thrown out of the vortex.

Although there are several ways to create photons, in the hydrogen atom, a photon is part of the volume of three-dimensional space flowing from the electron to the proton. When certain conditions occur, the vortex shortens, throwing a packet of condensed three-dimensional space back into the three-dimensional space from whence it came.

What is very important, is the photon's velocity. The velocity of the photon is the velocity of the vortex. Consequently, the speed of light can now be traced to the speed of the vortex!

Although the present vision of the universe states that the photon "instantaneously" travels at the speed of light, we can now see that this is not true at all. It can readily be seen that a photon is but a part of the volume of three-dimensional space that was already circulating at the speed of light before it was thrown free of the atom.

These principles can all be seen in the following drawing:

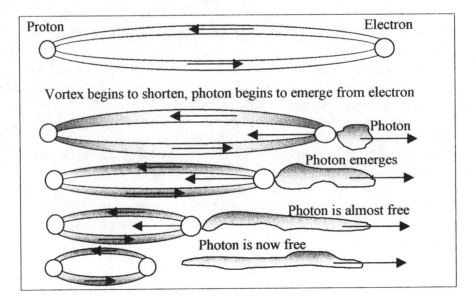

The photon can now be defined as a packet of condensed three-dimensional space, expanding and contracting in a long tubular shape perpendicular to its direction of travel. The rate of its expansion and contraction – or frequency - is a direct function of the volume of condensed space within the photon. The particle effects of the photon are a direct result of its being a condensed packet of three-dimensional space, while its wave effects are created by the expansion and then the contraction of the three-dimensional space it is passing through. And just as before, using the principles of "less dense and flowing space", another one of science's greatest mysteries - the particle and wave effect of light - is easily explained!

(The reason why the photon expands and contracts will be explained in the second book of this three part series.)

If I was excited before, I was ecstatic now! I had united three parts of the universe that, up until now, were three separate and individual pieces. I was getting closer, I was closing in on the ultimate and final vision of the universe. However, I still had a big problem - the neutron. How was the neutron constructed?

Although the neutron should be discussed in the section under matter, the discovery of the vortex had to be made before the amazing secret of the neutron could be unraveled. The words "amazing secret" were carefully chosen because what comes next is unlike anything anyone has ever seen before!

Ch17 THE SECRET OF THE NEUTRON!

The subatomic discoveries I had come across so far could be described as bizarre, fantastic, and unbelievable. But the next discovery tops even these descriptions.

It is easy to see how electrons and protons are three-dimensional holes. This discovery is revealed because their electrical charges are created by three-dimensional space flowing into or out of them. But the neutron has no charge. This means no space is flowing into it or out of it. So how can it be a hole?

The answer is that the neutron is not just one hole, it is a hole within a hole! A simply fantastic concept!

The neutron is created when an electron is shoved up against a proton and completely encircles it; or, the vortex flowing out of a proton into higher dimensional space is hit by the right type of "particle", breaks and completely encircles its three-dimensional surface. [This will be explained in great detail in book three of this three-part trilogy.]

Because the electron completely encircles the proton, the space flowing out of the electron is no longer flowing outward into the three-dimensional space of our universe. Instead, its direction is reversed. It is now flowing inwards, directly toward the three-dimensional hole (the proton) the electron is surrounding. This situation creates an enclosed loop.

The space flows out of the proton and into higher dimensional space; as soon as it does, it fans outward into a cone shape, is turned inside out, and instantly curls back upon itself creating a tight loop. This tight loop completes the return back into three-dimensional space by flowing directly onto the surface of the encircling electron, forming a fourth dimensional torus - or donut. A fantastic shape!

Perhaps even more fantastic than the shape of the neutron is its speed of circulation. This circulation is taking place within the shortest distance imaginable, yet moving at the incredible speed of 186,000 thousand miles a second!

The neutron has no charge because none of the space surrounding the neutron flows into it, or out of it.

Also, the higher dimensional vortex is bent into a very tight loop. In this tight loop, the vortex is turned inside out, creating the weak force of nature. Hence, the neutron's "neutral" charge, and the weak force of nature are both explained, clearing up two more of the great mysteries of nature!

Because this extraordinary creation of nature we call the Neutron is so unique, I have attempted to illustrate it in the following drawings. Unfortunately, since it is impossible to draw fourth-dimensional space, these two-dimensional to three-dimensional sketches are used:

INITIAL CONDITION:

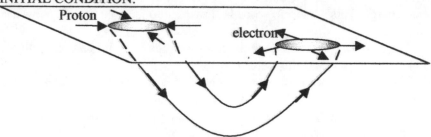

<u>STEP #1</u>, For any one of a number of possible reasons, the vortex breaks: [Note, this break is much closer to the surface than seen here.]

<u>STEP #2</u> Isolating the proton from the above drawing, and expanding its size, note how the bottom of the vortex begins to curl outward:

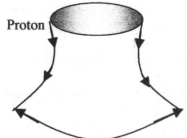

STEP #4 The curl becomes more pronounced and moves upward:

STEP #4 The vortex curls upward at an incredible speed towards the top of the hole we call the proton:

STEP #5 The vortex approaches the top of the hole called the proton:

STEP #6 The vortex curls back into the hole called the Proton, forms a torus, the circulating flow begins and becomes a new "particle" science calls the Neutron.

STEP #7 Another new "particle" called a *positron* is created when the end of the vortex attached to the electron reaches the two dimensional surface.

[Note how space flows into the hole called the positron; turning it into a "particle" with a charge opposite to that of the electron. (For those with a physics background, *the free end of the vortex now explains the creation of the phenomenon called Conservation of Charge! And another of the great mysteries of science is no more!)*]

Ch18 THE FOUR FORCES OF NATURE ARE FINALLY EXPLAINED!

Hallelujah I was on a roll!

Like the mysterious pieces of the ultimate jigsaw puzzle, the four parts of the universe were coming closer and closer together to reveal the ultimate vision of the universe. But it was a strange puzzle!

Instead of a jigsaw puzzle where you connect all of the pieces together, this was a puzzle where each piece somehow became something else! Where each time you connected two of them together, they disappeared into each other and became one - and you were always left with only one piece! It was a bizarre and perplexing experience. I didn't care.

It was the thrill of a lifetime! I was doing what no man had ever done before and would never do again. I was going to be the first person in all of human history, to "see it all!" And I was almost there.

I was very close to the "top of the mountain" where I could finally "look over" and see everything in the physical universe! But there was one more obstacle to overcome - force: the four forces of nature.

After eliminating time, I had managed to unite matter, space, and energy. The only piece of the universe that was left was force - the four forces of nature.

Could they be united too?

Of the four forces, I realized I only had the strong force left to explain! Gravity was explained by the existence of less dense space between particles of matter. Einstein's hypothesis that bent space is equivalent to gravity is wrong. *It is less dense space that creates Gravity.* The bent space surrounding stars is itself a phenomenon - an effect - created by the spherical shell of less dense space surrounding large astronomical bodies.

The Electromagnetic force could be explained by flowing space; and the weak force could be explained by an inverted tight loop of flowing space. So it was a very good possibility that the strong force could be explained by some sort of configuration of *dense and flowing space** too.

So what was it?

Unfortunately, I had no idea.

For the first "time" in a long time, I was stumped. I had no answer and absolutely no idea of how to proceed.

---

* The term *dense and flowing space* is an abbreviation for *"dense or less dense and flowing space"*.

At a loss to know what to do, I decided to review what was known about force.

I again read how the 20th Century scientific vision of the universe sees the four forces of nature to be made of something called "Force". But what force is, or how or why it even exists is still unknown. [Although the Theory of Quantum Mechanics claims forces are passed back and forth between particles by other particles, the Graviton, a hypothetical particle supposed to carry the force of Gravity has not been discovered.]

I read how the creation of the forces of nature has long been one of the great mysteries of the universe. When Isaac Newton discovered Gravity, he called it a "force". Since then, three more "forces" were discovered. And many physicists believe these four forces are all manifestations of just one universal force, but they can't prove it.

I also reviewed how many scientists including Albert Einstein tried to unite the four forces into one universal force. But he, and everyone else who tried, failed miserably.

Of course I knew now why they had failed. None of them knew "time" was a false concept, nor did they know about the principles of less dense and flowing space. If they did, perhaps things might be different.

But none of this research seemed to help.

After spending a lot of effort researching the past failures of others, I was still getting nowhere. So I decided to try something else. I knew from studying quantum mechanics that the forces of nature are theorized to be the result of tiny particles. Thinking about the strong force and particles, I remembered something about a Japanese Physicist in the 1930s proposing that the strong force might be created by a "Virtual Particle" (an unseen particle being passed back and forth between the proton and the neutron).

However, from my knowledge of *dense and flowing space*, I knew such a particle would really be a three-dimensional hole in space.

Of course! That was it! That was it!

The key phrase was, "...being passed back and forth...!" Back and forth! That was it!

In the blink of an eye, I solved the problem. And it was simple! It was so simple a child could understand it!

As you recall, the proton is a three-dimensional hole surrounded by a spherical region of space bent into it, and even though the neutron is a combination of a hole within a hole, it is also surrounded by a spherical region of space bent into it.

When a neutron approaches a proton, these two depressions in space try to bend into each other. When they do, some of the space flowing out of the spherical hole surrounding the neutron tries to flow into the proton that is beside it.

This situation would cause the enclosed vortex encircling the neutron to break free and encircle the opposite proton: turning *it* into the neutron while the one it vacated again becomes a proton. However, just as soon as the switch occurs, the process would begin all over again, causing it to reverse itself; the encircling vortex would break free of the proton it now surrounds, and return to the one it just left. It would keep on doing this dance, back and forth. Because this reversal happens so incredibly fast, this dancing hole of space would end up keeping one "particle" pressed tightly against the other - becoming the strong force of nature.

It should also be mentioned that since it is the invisible higher dimensional vortex that is first encircling one proton and then the other, from our perspective in three-dimensional space, this would look like a three-dimensional spherical particle is being passed back and forth!

Remarkable! Most remarkable!

This continual sharing or exchange of the three-dimensional hole surrounding the neutron becomes the Strong force of nature, explaining another of the great mysteries of science!

***** [Note: there could be a fifth force in nature created by the fourth dimensional volume within bosoms (proton like particles). When two of these particles collide, the attempt by three-dimensional space to form only one surface appears to be the reason why two positively charged particles can temporarily bond together forming the delta particle - a very short lived particle with a charge double that of a proton. However, this is speculation and will be covered in book three of this three-part trilogy.]

And suddenly there it was!

I had used the principles of *dense and flowing space* to explain the four forces of nature! And most wonderful of all, using the principles of *dense and flowing space*, the four forces of nature could now be united!

It was another great day in my life! A day I dreamed of and lived for! Everything in the universe, including the forces of nature could now be explained by the principles of *dense and flowing space*! Hallelujah, what a discovery! Hallelujah I was ecstatic!

But this was just a prelude. An anti-climax! Because the greatest discovery was yet to come, and it was even more spectacular because it was unforeseen - totally unexpected!

Ch19 THE SHOCKING TRUTH ABOUT FORCE!

Ever since Isaac Newton got hit on the head by an apple falling from a tree and discovered gravity, the world has had to deal with the presence of a mysterious unseen "force". This force called Gravity causes matter to accelerate towards other matter. Even when we are standing still upon the seemingly motionless surface of this planet, the molecules within our bodies are constantly being accelerated towards it. We call this acceleration our weight. It is this acceleration that holds us upon the surface of this spinning sphere and keeps us from flying off into space.

Because of the above facts, we live with force every day. Force is with us every second of our worldly lives.

Because three more forces were eventually discovered, the word "force" has become a casual part of our vocabulary. We use this word freely and easily even though we don't realize that the creation of force is still a total and complete mystery! [Even the highly accepted and widely believed explanations proposed in Quantum Mechanics is a mistake as we shall soon see.] Although we all believe in force, nobody [until now] knows how it is being generated!

Although at one time, nobody in the entire world knew about the force of gravity, today, there is perhaps nobody in the world that does not know about it. It is another one of those very few commonly shared beliefs accepted among all the men of this planet.

I know because nobody believed in gravity more fervently than I. Before I undertook this journey of discovery, I believed that force was a mysterious energy or substance surrounding matter, binding it together.

Because of this misconception, it took a while before I finally realized the shocking truth about force! Just like the "shocking truth" about matter, space, time, and energy is like nothing we have ever imagined before, so is force:

The shocking truth about "force" is that it just doesn't exist!

The reason why nobody can explain what force is or how it is being generated comes from the fact that the universe contains no mysterious "substance" called force. Nor are there any subatomic particles that "carry force" with them as proposed in the Theory of Quantum Mechanics.

So just what creates force?

The creation of force begins with the expansion of three-dimensional space.

On the universal, or massive scale, space is expanding outwards in all three dimensions at once. But on the microscopic scale, tiny regions of space are flowing backward, in the opposite direction to space's massive outward expansion. Like miniature eddy currents, space is flowing backwards into protons, in the direction of higher dimensional space.

What is the cause of this backward flow?

This backward flow of space is the result of higher dimensional space being unable to expand outward as rapidly as its surface. [The explanation for this condition will be given in Book Two of this three part series.] This inability causes it to "pull" backwards upon three-dimensional space. This backward pull creates the indentations or holes in the surface of three-dimensional space we call protons. Three-dimensional space flows backward, through these holes and into higher dimensional space, returning again to the three-dimensional surface via another three-dimensional hole - the electron.

Because no other terminology seems appropriate to describe this phenomenon, it can be called an "inter-dimensional force". It creates drag on space, makes it flow backwards, and produces four different conditions that distort the spherical shape of the three-dimensional holes. It is the straightening out of these distortions that produce the accelerations that are misinterpreted as forces.

If the great scientists of the 20th Century (including Einstein) who tried to unite the forces, were able to see exactly how the universe is constructed; they would be astonished to learn that there are no "forces" of nature! They were trying to unite something that doesn't exist!

What we call force is merely a condition created by dense and flowing space that causes the normal spherical shape of particles to distort into "pear shapes". These pear shapes are unnatural bends. This unnatural bend creates a surface tension that tries to straighten itself back into a sphere. As it does, the sphere (hole) moves slightly in the direction of the other hole. However, as soon as it starts to straighten out, it is again distorted, repeating the process, making it move faster and faster, accelerating the particle towards the other hole. [Note, in the case of the Electrostatic Repulsive Force, the direction of the distortion is reversed, and the particles move away from each other.]

When we stand upon this planet, the shape of every proton, electron, and neutron is distorted towards the Earth's center. The collective attempt of these particles to straighten, pushes us towards the surface of the Earth and becomes the "force" we identify as our weight.

Normal shape   Normal shape

Length #1

When close together or in a massive region of less dense space (powerful gravitational field), the spherical shape distorts into a pear shape:

Distorted shape   Distorted shape

At the point of the pear, space is sharply bent. As it tries to straighten back into a spherical hole, the backside of each hole moves towards the point. This motion shifts each sphere towards the other, accelerating them.

Length #2

However, as soon as they become spheres, they distort and the process happens all over again:

As the process of distortion and reshaping repeats itself, note how length #2 becomes shorter than length #1. This change in distance represents the motion of these two holes as they move towards each other. The density of space determines how fast they accelerate towards each other.

   Note: although this entire process will be explained in greater depth in book two of this three part trilogy, a little thought will enable anyone to figure out how this same process works with the other three "forces". Also, a little more thought will explain why a hole surrounded with space *bent outward* is *also* accelerated towards a region of less dense space!

   The knowledge of the creation of the phenomenon of force is the fourth and final piece of the puzzle. It is the union of these four pieces that completes the picture and finally allows us to see the ultimate vision of the universe:

   When I first saw the true vision of the universe, the vision that no man has ever seen before, I was awestruck! Thunderstruck!

This true vision of the universe is the greatest discovery ever made! It is a shocker! A blockbuster!

Stated simply, there are no separate "parts" to the universe!
There is only space and its motion! [And that's it!]
The only thing that exists in the physical universe is the substance of which space is made. Space is not "space" at all. Space is made of something that is totally unique from our point of view. It is constructed out of at least five dimensions, and it can both bend and flow.

This substance is in motion. It is moving in two opposite directions at once: on a massive scale, it is expanding outward at an incredible speed carrying the Galaxies with it. But on the microscopic scale, like the eddy currents in a river, it is flowing backwards at an equally incredible speed (from our point of view)!

Both matter and energy are created out of space. The "particles" of matter - protons, electrons, and neutrons - [and a host of other "particles"] are not particles at all. They are three-dimensional holes existing upon the surface of fourth-dimensional space. The substance of which space is made flows into and out of these holes. The hole creates a particle effect, while the denser or less dense space surrounding the hole creates a wave effect.

Energy is also created out of dense and flowing space. Energy in the form of photons, are really denser regions of space that expand and contract as they move. This dense region - or photon - creates a particle effect, while the expansion and contraction of the space it passes through creates a wave effect.

Time does not exist; the phenomenon of time is created throughout the universe by the uniform flow of microscopic space into and out of the three-dimensional holes of matter.

There are NO "forces" of nature! Using the massive expansion of three-dimensional space throughout the universe as a reference, its backward flow into the tiny microscopic holes is responsible for the creation of four special, though uniform configurations of dense and flowing space. These uniform configurations distort the spherical surfaces of the three-dimensional holes, accelerating them towards each other, creating the illusion of force!

Ch20 AT LAST - THE ALPHA AND THE OMEGA

When seen for the first time, the vision of our incredibly diverse and complex universe being created out of only one substance is a shocker! And yet strangely, for the first time in many years, it also left me feeling calm and at peace with myself.

At long last the awful feeling of not knowing the answers and the helplessness of not being able to find the answers was gone. I had finally freed myself from the curse of ignorance that possesses the entire human race.

I had crawled out of the abyss. I had gone where no man has ever gone before, and I had seen the vision of the universe that no man has ever seen before.

But what had I seen? And even more important, what does it mean?

Like Columbus of old, had I stumbled unto a brand new world while trying to find the old East Indies?

Indeed I had!

The above discovery is so revolutionary there is nothing to compare it to. It stands alone and apart from all of the other knowledge in the world. *It is the beginning and the end, the Alpha and the Omega of discoveries!*

Everything that exists, every physical relationship, even the creation of the universe itself can be explained by this vision. [The creation of the physical universe will be explained in book two of this three part series.} Hence, the ultimate vision of the universe is also - *"The Theory of Everything" The Rosetta stone of science!*

This vision also possesses a delicate elegance unique unto itself. Its wonderful simplicity surrounds it with an aura of beauty, unlike anything ever seen before.

To grasp the incredible implications of this vision, first look at or visualize all of the different colors you can see or think of. Look at the reds, the blues, the yellows, the greens, and all of the myriad numbers of colors in-between - and then realize that they are all made out of just one "color"! Just one!

Next, visually imagine anything and everything you can think of. Think of the forests, the mountains, the deserts, the oceans, the white clouds in the deep blue sky, or the twinkling stars in the dark night sky and realize that this incredible diversity of shapes, sizes and textures are all made out of just one shape! It is a humbling and profound experience.

But there is even a more profound experience: look around the room you are sitting in. Look at all of the different and separate things you see including *yourself.* Now look again at these separate objects and realize that *these are not separate objects at all!*

EVERYTHING YOU SEE, INCLUDING YOURSELF, IS ONE THING! THERE ARE NO SEPARATE PARTS!

SEPERATION IS AN ILLUSION! IT IS AN ILLUSION CREATED BY THE FACT THAT WE CANNOT SEE THE MATERIAL SPACE IS MADE OF. WE ONLY SEE THE HOLES AND NOT THE MATERIAL BETWEEN THE HOLES!

EVERYTHING THAT EXISTS EVERYWHERE WITHIN THE PHYSICAL UNIVERSE, INCLUDING EVERY ONE OF US, IS MADE OF ONE SUBSTANCE!

WE ARE ALL ONE WITH IT. WE ALL MOVE WITHIN IT! WE ALL EXIST WITHIN IT!

Wow!.....Wow! Wow! Wow! Wow! Wow!

I wish I could adequately express all of my feelings when I discovered this ultimate vision of the universe, but any effort seems inadequate. Someone once said that man's creations pale beside the works of God. And no truer statement was ever made.

This vision of the universe is also peaceful. The amazing complexity of the physical universe being created by something so incredibly simple is comforting and reassuring. In fact, the more you think about it the calmer you will become. Try it yourself.

The next time you are stuck in rush hour traffic on the freeway, imagine the peacefulness and the stillness of the substance of which everything you see around you is imbedded. Imagine its quietness, its calmness, even as the chaos of matter seethes *within it.*

When I first did it, it was as if I was at one with the universe; it was meditation; it was the OM: it was a religious experience. A most profound religious experience!

(A most profound religious experience!) Wait a minute! A most profound religious experience?

What does this mean?

What was I really looking at?

What had I found?

Is it...is it God?

Ch21 IS THIS GOD? HAVE WE DISCOVERED GOD?

A great philosopher once said, "Know thyself".

I guess I never knew myself until I asked myself the question, "Is this God?" because when I did, I was suddenly afraid!

Just what had I stumbled onto?

I was just a mental adventurer in search of the thoughts no man had ever thought before. But never, never in my wildest dreams, did I ever even think I might discover God!

Had I?

How can such a question even be answered? How *would* anyone know if they had discovered God? How *could* anyone know if they discovered God?

Is there any way to recognize God? How can God be identified? What is the definition of God?

Looking in the Bible for a description of God we see terms such as the *"Alpha and the Omega"*, and the *"I am, That I am"*.

Using these terms, it is easy to see that the substance out of which space is made is certainly the Alpha and the Omega, the beginning and the end of everything that exists in the physical universe, but is it the "I am, that I am" of the Bible?

Just what is it? Is there a way to find out?

Grateful for the opportunity to turn my mind to another subject, I looked for a way to resolve this dilemma. And while thinking about it, I realized that the answer could be found in the creation of the universe.

I realized that if God created the universe, there are three ways he could have done it: the universe is created out of God; the universe is a unique manifestation of God; or the universe itself is a creation of God.

If the universe is created out of God, the space of the universe is God, and we exist within the actual physical body of God. This vision is comparable to the existence of a single biological cell living within our physical body. (A single microscopic creature existing within a much larger, massive creature!)

If the universe is a unique manifestation of God, the space of the universe might be a thought and we might be mental projections within this thought form. Although this idea might seem farfetched, we must never forget that we dream. In our dreams we appear to see real images, and have real experiences. [How does this happen, how are these images formed, and why do they appear so real?]

But if the universe itself is a creation of God, then space is a creation of God, and we are creations within the creation. This scenario can be compared to a man inventing a liquid plastic, forming bubbles within its volume, and then somehow arranging the bubbles to form images.

So which is which?

Another question: can a mere mortal man even answer such a question? Are there limits to the mental constructs our mind is capable of forming?

The mental picture of God being indescribable and incomprehensible to the mind of a mere man is one of the accepted beliefs of world religion. But is it true? Can a creation analyze its creator? Was it a sin to even try?

But then again, maybe it would be a sin to not try. Maybe I was reacting to the inherited fears of our ancient ancestors. The same fears that kept them from crossing the ocean because they were all afraid they were going to fall off of the edge of the world. Or the fears that kept them from challenging the hypocritical doctrine of the church leaders, and allowing the inquisition to take place because they believed these maniacal priests were doing the will of God.

In the past, men also believed in demons. They tortured, and murdered other men in fear of them. However, they failed to realize that the only real demons were the fear and ignorance within their own minds.

Fear and ignorance, ignorance and fear! The true rulers of men! Allowed to run rampant and without restraint they accentuate each other, intensify each other, until they dominate the minds of men.

But no matter how powerful they seem, they are only thoughts. Because they are only thoughts, the way to beat them is with another thought or with no thought at all. To totally ignore their presence!

And that is exactly what I did. I told myself that my fears were mental projections put into my mind by ignorant men and gave them no more credence. Then, I boldly returned to the subject of the moment: is the space of the universe God?

While thinking about it, I began to recall all of the religious texts of the world. I remembered that wherever men believed in God there seemed to be three words that everyone everywhere in the world agreed upon. Three words that are universally accepted and associated with God in all religious beliefs. These words are *omnipresent, omniscient, and omnipotent.* They speak for themselves:

If the substance out of which space is made is God, then God is surely *omnipresent.* God is everywhere. Every "particle" of matter and every photon of energy everywhere in the physical universe is made out of him. Since he would be aware of every motion of everything that exists everywhere in the universe, he would know "when a single sparrow falls from the sky". He would also know the configurations and the interconnections of every neuron within a man's mind. He would know when electrical current flows between them, and in doing so, he would know every thought a man thinks!

Knowing every thought a man thinks, there would be no fooling God. He would know the hypocrisy, the lies, and the true feelings of every man in the world. Knowing all and seeing all, he would know the secrets of every person everywhere in the universe.

He would know when a man earnestly prayed to be heard by him, or to really be seen by other men. He would know what happens in the light of day or in the darkest dungeon in the world. His knowledge would be all encompassing, and universal. He would indeed be *omniscient*.

However, is he *omnipotent?*

It is easy to see how the substance out of which space is made is omnipresent, and omniscient, but to be omnipotent is another matter entirely.

The deep contemplation of this problem reveals that the key to its answer is found in motion. The creation of the universe began when space was put into motion. But did space set *itself* into motion, or did something else do it?

If something else set it into motion, it is not omnipotent and it is not God. However, if the substance out of which space is made set itself into motion, then *it* created the universe out of itself. It made everything, and in doing so, became omnipotent.

To be omnipotent, means it had the ability to create the universe and used that ability. This shows premeditation and cognizance of thought. Which means space had to have the ability to both think and reason before the physical universe was created.

However, all of these ideas are all predicated upon the premise that space possesses awareness - consciousness! Does it?

While thinking of a way to answer this question, surprisingly, the following answer seemed to just pop into my mind all by itself. It begins like this:

Where does our awareness - our consciousness - come from? In fact, where does any animal's awareness come from?

If we could take a human being apart, atom by atom, we would find that we would have several thousand piles of compounds. If we could then break these compounds apart and separate them into the individual elements they are constructed out of, we would have about a hundred piles of individual elements. And finally, if we could take these individual elements apart, we would end up with three big piles of electrons, protons, and neutrons.

But these are inanimate objects! They possess no consciousness or awareness. Furthermore, all three of these piles are not "matter" at all. They are just three massive collections of three-dimensional holes in space. So we are left with a stunning conclusion: a particular arrangement of three-dimensional holes creates consciousness!

And something even more fantastic: the inanimate objects of the universe have obtained consciousness of themselves! When *we* look at a proton or an electron, in reality, it is the matter of the universe that is looking back at itself! A simply astounding idea!

And it is this astounding idea that leads us to another even more astonishing idea: if a creation made out of nothing but holes in space can obtain consciousness of itself, can the space it is created out of obtain consciousness of itself too?

If it can, and if it set itself into motion creating the physical universe - and us in the process - then my friends, it is God!

PART III

Ch22 THE SEARCH FOR A PROOF BEGINS

There are a lot of mental discoveries that ignite and booster our excitement. But the possibility of finding God had the opposite effect upon me. I became wary of myself. Had I gone a "bridge too far" in this mental journey? Was I mad?

I needed to get back to reality (whatever that is). Although the question that space possesses consciousness is not rhetorical, it does not appear to be provable or "disprovable" either. I know because I tried to think of every way possible to do it. Afterwards, I knew it was time to return to the beginning.

After realizing I had finally come to the end of a simply wonderful chain of revolutionary discoveries, I knew I needed to return my attention to higher dimensional space. Because of all the shocking discoveries I had made, perhaps the most shocking of all was the fact that I couldn't believe any of it - yet!

I had accumulated a lot of circumstantial evidence for the existence of higher dimensional space. Metaphorically speaking, I had gone where no man has gone before. I had stood upon the mountain, and had seen the wonders of the universe the world's greatest philosophers, scientists, and wise men have only dreamt of seeing.

I felt privileged and humbled. But it was all for nothing unless I could prove it!

Although I desperately wanted to believe in higher dimensions where the Kingdom of God existed, where souls existed as souls, and where peace, joy, love, and happiness reigns supreme forever and ever, I knew I couldn't believe any of it unless I had proof. Just like the Disciple Thomas who had to see the holes in Jesus' hands before he could believe, I needed proof too! And to convince me that Heaven existed, I was going to have to see one Hell of a proof!

And here is where I became really tough upon myself. Because not only did this proof have to reveal the Vortex Theory was true - it also had to prove the Vortex Theory was equal to – and equivalent to the Theory of Relativity. It had to show the Vortex Theory explained the bizarre phenomenon of the universe just as well as the Theory of Relativity.

This meant I was going to have to somehow use the Vortex Theory to explain the "granddaddy" of all the special effects in the universe – the length shrinkage, and time dilation effects which occur at near light velocities.

To accomplish this seemingly impossible feat, I was going to have to come up with a mathematical explanation for the way atoms shrank and the phenomenon of time slowed down when travelling at near light velocities. To do this, I was first going to have to discover the mechanics of how and why the vortices flowing between the protons and electrons shrank when atoms begin to move!

Simply put, I had to do what no man had ever done before, I had to successfully find another explanation for the most difficult problem man has ever encountered in his exploration of the universe. I also knew there would only be me to do it. I would not get any help from anybody else.

Faced with the enormity of such a problem, I was temporarily overwhelmed.

My god what a problem! Why did it have to fall to me? Who was I? I was not an engineer or a mathematician. I was a construction worker. I built pools for a living. I didn't solve complicated math problems anymore.

Math problems! This was no ordinary math problem. The true explanation of the Michelson Morley Experiment was a world class math problem. It was the Olympic Games of math problems. People won Nobel prizes for solving math problems such as this one! Men who are now legends in the world of science were the ones who made the previous explanations of this experiment and there were also many other legends in the world of science that were incapable of solving it.

But then I had another thought.

Although such a task might seem like the impossible dream for a construction worker, I knew that if the Vortex Theory was the correct explanation for the construction of the universe, the proof already existed; it was already there, just waiting to be discovered.

So I had nothing to fear. If the Vortex Theory was correct, it would explain exactly how the length of objects shrank, and how the phenomenon of "time" slowed down when travelling at near light velocities.

I had traveled a long way using that little quote from Jesus in the New Testament. It would be a pity to quit now.

Since I had found the rest, I made up my mind I would find the proof too; I made up my mind I was going to succeed; that I had already succeeded. Besides, if I was right, how could I fail? So get going Russell.

What's your problem! Hang in there buddy! Don't quit! Never give up! Never! Never! Never!

(Reluctantly, I set out to find the answer.)

Little did I know it would take seven more years!

Seven more difficult and frustrating years!

Many times I tried and failed. But I never quit; I never lost faith that I would succeed. I kept on and on, until eventually, I triumphed. And it was a wonderful success.

Using that little quote made by Jesus in the New Testament, I discovered one of the most beautiful and elegant mathematical relationships in all of nature. I discovered mechanical movements of the vortices taking place within atoms that are so precise and so exact that there is nothing in our contemporary world to compare them to. And it was in the mathematical relationships and mechanical movements of these vortices that I discovered exactly how matter shrinks, and how the motions of matter slow down - making it appear as if "time" itself has somehow slowed down.

I found out that the length shrinkage and time dilation effects occurring at near light velocities are created by a phenomenon that can be called THE SLOWER APPARENT VELOCITY of *dense and flowing space*. The mathematics of the slower apparent velocity is explained in the APPENDIX.

I also discovered that these same relationships extend to individual particles, making the *dense and flowing space* they are created out of, shrink and move slower too.

These wonderful explanations finally allowed me to deduce the true explanation for the Michelson Morley Experiment. The true explanation of this most important of all scientific experiments proves the existence of higher dimensional space – which proves that two thousand years ago Jesus knew more about the construction of the universe than all of the greatest scientists who have ever lived!

This proof can be found in THE APPENDIX.

Although the mathematics and the formulas contained within the body of this proof only take a High School level of math to understand, I also realize that most folks are not interested in these technical details. (For anyone that is, any High School math teacher possesses the ability to explain this proof.)

It should also be mentioned that this proof was just the beginning of many more wonderful discoveries. These discoveries were so numerous they take up a book of their own. Hence, all but one of them will be published in the second book of this three part series.

The one discovery that needs to be mentioned here is so important that it cannot wait. This discovery explains one of the greatest secrets of the universe - *the secret of time* - the secret of how the phenomenon of time is created! This secret is explained at the end of this section.

Ch23 WHAT DOES IT ALL MEAN?

The end of the era of time is the end of the longest and most enduring era in all of human history.

Although "time" was just an idea, the end of time is not just the end of an idea; it is the end of a way of life. Over the countless millennia that time has been a part of the collective consciousness of man, the entire culture of the human race has become tied to this concept, and everything that can be thought of is affected by its demise.

The end of the era of time affects all of science, technology, philosophy, and religion. Because these four subjects encompass every field of human endeavor, the lives of every person in every culture and in every country in the world will be directly affected.

As previously mentioned, every science book in the world is now obsolete. Equally shocking is the fact that every school, college, and university is teaching all of their students scientific knowledge that is totally and completely wrong!

All of the teachers, engineers, and technicians in the world need to be reeducated and retrained. But when they are, they will not only encounter the revolutionary knowledge that will allow them to see the ultimate vision of the universe, they will also encounter the following dilemma:

"In an age when there were no scientists or scientific experiments, how did Jesus possess the scientific knowledge of the universe which no man in the world knew until now? Not just any knowledge, but knowledge of the actual existence of higher dimensional space! Knowledge which is perhaps the most difficult of all the scientific knowledge of the universe to acquire, because it can only be proven after the acquisition of a long chain of other scientific discoveries!

Also, it is very important to know that the existence of higher dimensional space is not some sort of low priority subject; without the presence of higher dimensional space, NOTHING within the three dimensional universe would exist! There would be no three dimensional vortices extending into higher dimensional space. Because there would be no three-dimensional holes there would be no protons, electrons, or atoms. Consequently, higher dimensional space is not some

99

insignificant place existing in a little corner of the cosmos. It is
the most important place in the entire universe. Without higher
dimensional space there is no universe, no stars, no Earth, and
no us!

Furthermore, the discovery of the existence of higher
dimensional space and the remarkable chain of scientific
discoveries that followed; all resulted from the words of Jesus
in the NEW TESTAMENT. Without the words of Jesus, these
discoveries would never have been made!

There is no denying the above fact or escaping from it. One quote,
spoken by a supposedly "disgruntled Jewish philosopher", has suddenly
turned the logic of science upon itself! Just like a sun-burnt scorpion
stings itself to death, the very principles of science, which once turned
men against the belief in God, will now turn men against the "scientific
atheism" these principles were responsible for creating.

The circle is now complete – science has discovered the "Backdoor" to
the Kingdom of God!

Although it will take some time for this astounding conclusion to
become part of the collective consciousness of man, when it finally does,
something amazing will have occurred. A scientific revolution will have
sweep through the churches of the world, and a religious revolution will
have swept through every scientific center of learning in the world.

Each will complement the other, and together, the whole will become
greater than the sum of its parts! And just as the intellectuals of the past
rejected Jesus, the intellectuals of the future will accept Jesus. Perhaps
they will make the world a better place. But one thing is for sure, they
will be faced with one of the greatest philosophical problems ever to
confront mankind: do we exist within the body of God?

EPILOGUE

Many years had passed since I read that story in *Readers Digest*. I had come a long way. I had discovered the ultimate knowledge of the universe; and I had found a way to prove it to even my skeptical mind. But when I tried to give it to the world, I ran into the ultimate "Catch 22".

Because I refused to edit the words *God* and *Jesus* from the math, no physicist would even look at it. Because I could not get the backing of "physicists", no science journal would publish this work. [And even if they would, I was told that none of them would allow any religious connotations to be a part of an article in one of "their" journals.]

Because I could not get a science journal to publish my work, no newspaper or science oriented magazine would do an article on it. Without a panel of physicists to tell them the math was right, they were afraid of making fools of themselves by telling the world a construction worker found a mistake in Einstein's Theory of Relativity.

Television and radio were out. I contacted stations, and took my work to them, but they refused for the same reasons. And I would not degrade the words of Jesus by going on one of the daytime talk shows, so what to do?

Thinking about the problem and knowing that there must be other people like me in the world who desperately wanted to know the answers but had no way to find them, I finally decided to write a book.

However, thinking about writing a book, and actually writing it, are two different matters.

Because I have trouble just writing letters, it was a long drawn out process. After months of working on it at night and on weekends, I finished a primitive version, made ten copies and gave it to ten friends to read.

Because they were friends, they all told me, "Yall, its great. It's terrific! I really enjoyed it, really!" But the look on their faces told the true story.

It wasn't very good.

Troubled and disappointed I said, "To hell with it! To hell with it all! Who even cares about the truth? If men choose to be dumb, let them be dumb! I'm finished with them!"

So I sat the book aside and forgot about it.

But I didn't know that other forces were still at work!

About six months later, on a Sunday afternoon, I was driving east on Sheridan Boulevard in Fort Lauderdale, Florida. I was in my old pickup truck, heading back to my apartment on Hollywood beach, when a wheel bearing went out on the right front wheel.

Because all of the garages are closed on Sunday, I knew I could not get it repaired until Monday. Also, if I had it towed to where I lived, it would be very difficult or impossible to work on it in my narrow parking space. So my next thought was to think about where I could keep it overnight.

Everyone I knew lived on the other side of town, except for Donna. Donna only lived about two miles away, and she was one of the people I had given the manuscript to.

I had known her for many years. Her late husband and I used to be partners, and I knew she wouldn't mind helping out. I called her up and she said, "of course it was all right". So, I called a tow truck. This %&%$*# charged me fifty dollars to make the ten minute trip and I was boiling mad.

But Donna is a jewel. Always optimistic, always easy-going, she told me she was glad I wasn't in a wreck and to, "forget about the truck driver."

She then changed the subject by saying that some friends of hers from England, who were staying there for a few days and were out at the moment would be back soon. So I got out my tools, jacked up the truck, and started taking off the front wheel when a jeep pulled into the driveway.

A man and a woman got out. I recognized the man as Paolo, but the woman I had never seen before. Although she was plainly dressed, there was something very attractive about her. She had a warm and friendly smile and appeared to be about my age. I liked her the moment I saw her.

Donna came out and introduced Paolo's friend Jeannie to me. Paolo offered to drive me down to a parts place to get a new bearing and the truck was soon fixed.

So we both went into the back yard where Donna and Jeannie were seated at a table, and sat down. After some small conversation had taken place between the four of us for a few minutes, Paolo and Donna got up from the table to move some roofing material stored on her porch.

So I turned to Jeannie and asked her what she thought of America. She told me it was a wonderful country. She explained how Paolo and his wife Giuliana were good friends of hers. About how she wanted to attend a healing conference in Tucson Arizona, but didn't want to go alone. That she enjoyed being in America, thought it was a great country and was sad that she was going home tomorrow. And then she said something odd:

She said she was sorry she was leaving because she had read a wonderful manuscript on "Time" just before she left England, and would have liked to meet the author before she went home.

She began to describe it, and as she did, it sounded exactly like my book! I couldn't believe it!

Surprising her, (and myself), I suddenly got up from the table, went out to my truck and came back with a copy of the manuscript and put it down on the table.

"Was this the book?"

"Yes, that's it! That's the one I read!"

"Well, I'm the guy who wrote it!"

We just sat there staring at each other.

I would like to have said something to her, but I was confused. Just how did she get a copy of my book and how did it get to England?

But I soon forgot about the book.

The more I looked at Jeannie, and the more she looked at me, it was as if we were old friends.

When Donna and Paolo came back to the table, and they both heard the story, Paolo confessed that he was the one who had taken the book to England.

Six months before, when he was visiting Donna, he had seen the copy of the manuscript on her desk. He had looked at it, found it interesting, and since he couldn't buy one, had made a Xerox copy of it. He had taken it to England and shown it to his wife and some friends, including Jeannie. But she was the only one who had actually read it!

We were all amazed.

Jeannie asked me when I was going to have it published and I told her I was fed up with the book. I told her how everyone who was capable of understanding the mathematical proof was ignoring it because I was a construction worker who was inspired by the words of Jesus in the New Testament.

I told her that it would probably never be published.

But later that evening we had a chance to talk again in private.

She insisted that it was too important a work to let die. She said I had to get it out to the people of the world because they needed it to overcome the atheistic attitudes that dominate present day science. That God needs to be put back into the scientific equations that explain the workings of the universe! That the very people who think they don't need it, are the very people who need it the most, and that just like the "me" of many years ago, they need this knowledge to regain their faith in God too!

I answered her by asking what she did. She said she was an impressionistic painter.

(Again I was surprised because I simply love impressionistic paintings.)

I asked her if I could see some of her art?

She said yes.

She had a folder full of her work, showed it to me, and I was impressed.

After looking at all of it, I told her that the theme of her paintings was "Peace and love".

She smiled and said, "Peace, Love, Joy and Harmony!" Then we both smiled at each other.

One painting I really liked a lot. I asked her if I published the book could I use it on the cover. She took it out of the folder and gave it to me. Ten months later, we were married.

Our friends said it was meant to happen. Everyone who has heard the story is amazed at the incredible synchronicity of the events that occurred on that day.

They all keep marveling about it. What if I hadn't been driving on that particular road; or what if the truck had broken down any other place; or what if she had not been there on that one day, we would never have met. Even more incredible, she wanted to meet me, and I miraculously appeared!

But I have another idea: it was another one of those events necessary to make the people of the world aware of the knowledge within this book. Without her, this book would have died.

She urged me on. She is the one responsible for having this book published. I would never have done it if it hadn't been for her.

As I look back at my life, it is almost as if I was an invisible pawn being pushed secretly across some massive chessboard in a mighty chess game between science and religion. An invisible pawn that suddenly appears at the end of the game, surprises the opposition, and checkmates the dark king of atheistic science!

And when I say I was pushed, I mean pushed! When I tried to quit, I was not allowed to quit. Every possible obstacle I encountered was overcome by me or for me. And when I was down and out in the last round of the fight, and thought I was finished, someone miraculously appeared, gave me a hand up, and urged me onward. Ever onward! It is almost as if God wants the people of the world to know these ultimate and final truths about the universe and won't settle for anything less!

Perhaps He is fed up with the self appointed judges of the world: those skeptical scientists - and priests - who try to tell other men that God and Science are two different subjects. That there is no place for God in a science book, and no place for science in religious studies!

But no longer is this for other men to decide. Although the world is filled with judges, who try to dictate to others what they should or shouldn't believe, they are not the jury. You are!

You are responsible for what you choose to believe. You have the final say. When the trial is over, you are the ones who are given the evidence and asked to retire from the courtroom to consider the truth.

And that is what you must do now. My work is over. But yours has just begun.

Is it the truth? The only way to tell is through the mathematical proof.

Even though it only takes a High School level of mathematics to understand the proof, I know that many people are uncomfortable with mathematics. If you are one who is, don't worry.

Ask a High School math teacher to look at it. If you have a child in school, ask him or her to take it to their teacher. What can it hurt?

Besides, isn't it worth it to find out if you are paying money for education's that are worthless? Isn't it worth it to find out if public schools are teaching your children science that is totally and completely wrong?

Many people in many different generations wanted to change the world; and many people would like to see the world change into a better place. But almost everyone who has wanted to had no way of doing it. Until now!

Everyone of you who has read this book now holds the power. The proof within this manuscript is no ordinary proof. It possesses the power to change the world. It is the hammer of God. It pounds the opposition to pieces.

It will put God back in the public schools. A public school is where the revolution will begin. And then it will spread.

Just imagine a New Testament in every *science* classroom in every school in every state of the United States! Bibles put in classrooms by the Supreme Court in response to the demand by *one person or parent* that their child be taught the science that was discovered (and proved) via the words of Jesus in the New Testament! Oh! I can hardly wait! I can hardly wait! *REMEMBER, IT ONLY TAKES ONE PERSON!*

One of you will do it. One of you reading this book will begin the sequence of events that will eventually change all of mankind. HOORAY FOR YOU WHOEVER YOU ARE!

The End

THE APPENDIX

THE PROOF

In *THE END OF THE CONCEPT OF "TIME"*, a revolutionary new vision of the universe was introduced. The "five pieces" of the universe - Matter, Space, Time, Energy, and the forces of nature are not constructed in the way 20th Century science presently believes. They exist in a manner unlike anything anyone has ever imagined before. Like a world turned upside down, nothing is as it appears.

Matter, instead of being made of something, is made of nothing; Space, instead of being made of nothing, is made of something; Time doesn't exist, "Force" doesn't exist, while Energy and four "Forces of Nature" are constructed out of *dense and flowing space!* In fact, *everything in the universe is made out of only one substance – space!* *["Space" is not Space!]*

But most important of all, these ideas are not speculation. They are backed up by an exact mathematical proof.

The proof of this revolutionary new vision of the universe is found in its precise mathematical explanation for the length shrinkage and time dilation effects associated with the Michelson Morley Experiment. Named the Vortex Theory, this new vision of the universe will first prove why the length of matter parallel to the direction of travel shrinks; then it will prove why matter in the transverse direction to the velocity of travel does not shrink. And finally, it will give an exact mathematical explanation for the phenomenon of time dilation.

To accomplish this goal it is first necessary to summarize the major ideas proposed within this book – *THE END OF THE CONCEPT OF "TIME"* Book I

Summary of major ideas:
Using the Vortex Theory, the five pieces of the universe can be summarized as follows:

MATTER: the particles of matter we call protons and electrons are not particles at all. Instead they are 3d (three-dimensional) holes existing upon the surface of 4d (fourth-dimensional) space. Protons are 3d holes bent into 4d space, electrons are 3d holes bent out of 4d space, and neutrons are a combination of one 3d hole completely surrounding another 3d hole! (Quarks are theorized to be 4d holes existing upon the surface of 5d space.)

Atoms: When a proton captures an electron and becomes a hydrogen atom, these two holes are connected by two flowing vortices of 3d space. One vortex flows from the electron to the proton in 3d space, while the second flows out of the proton and back to the electron in fourth dimensional space.

SPACE: space is made of something. What this something is – is unknown. However, because it can bend and flow, it is speculated to be some sort of uniform congruent material unique from our point of view. (Note – this idea is not a return to the Aether Theory.)

TIME: time is a function of motion, a shadow of motion. Although the phenomenon of time exists, "time" doesn't! What man has called "time" for thousands of years is a phenomenon created by a hierarchy of motion. This hierarchy of motion starts with the velocity of the 3d space flowing within the vortices connecting "particles" together. All velocities of everything in the universe are functions of the velocity of these vortices and the elasticity of space. Even the speed of light is a function of the velocity of the space flowing within the vortices.

ENERGY: photons of light are condensed packets of 3d space traveling at the velocity of the vortices they are thrown from. These condensed packets of 3d space expand and contract perpendicular to their direction of travel.

THE FOUR FORCES OF NATURE: Force as some sort of *independent* manifestation of the universe doesn't exist. The four forces of nature – gravity, the electromagnetic force, the weak force, and the strong force are all created by *less dense, or more dense and flowing space*.

Important concepts:

Because the proof of this new vision of the universe involves some unusual principles, the following important concepts need to be understood.

THE NEED FOR SIMPLICITY: here it should be said that throughout this proof we must simplify our discussions. If we don't, we will become lost in trying to accomplish the almost impossible task of attempting to visualize the almost infinitesimal movements of atoms as they respond to the equally incomprehensibly large velocity of the speed of light.

To overcome this problem, it is easier to greatly increase the size of the atoms to diameters the mind feels more comfortable visualizing, while at the same time, greatly decreasing the speed of light to a value the mind has no problem comprehending.

Because the hydrogen atom is the simplest of all atoms, and the easiest to understand, it is the example used in the rest of this text. However, it must be understood that, just like the hydrogen atom, all protons and electrons in all atoms everywhere are connected by two vortices of flowing space. Therefore, the principles using the hydrogen atom as the example apply to all other atoms as well.

THE BACKDROP OF SPACE: In Einstein's Theory of Relativity, space was made of nothing and all motions were relative to each other and still are - for all practical, large scale human observations. However, in the Vortex Theory of matter, since space is made of something, all of the motions in the subatomic world are made in reference to the space immediately surrounding it. Even though over vast distances the proportions of 3d space are expanding, for very short distances, the expansion of 3d space is immaterial. Therefore, for the purposes of this discussion, 3d space can be considered to be at rest. As such, it is a reference referred to as the "BACK DROP OF SPACE" to which all motions in the subatomic world can be compared to.

THE PHENOMENON OF TIME AS A MEASURING TOOL: although the Vortex Theory proposes that time does not exist as a fundamental principle of the universe, the phenomenon of time can still be used as a measuring tool.

Because a clock uses or creates a harmonic motion, this harmonic motion can be used to measure the LENGTH between random motions. Hence, the use of time in the following formulas does not conflict with the original proposal.

THE ENCLOSED LOOP: when a proton captures an electron, the electromagnetic force pulls these two holes together creating a hydrogen atom. The space that flows into and out of them forms two vortices of flowing 3d (three-dimensional) space. 3d space, in the form of a vortex, flows from the electron through 3d space and into the proton. Then it flows out of the proton and into 4d (fourth dimensional) space. And finally, in the form of another 3d vortex, it flows back through 4d space to the electron, completing the circuit.

This circulation creates an ENCLOSED LOOP. The circulating flow begins, and the volume of flowing, 3d space within the two vortices remains trapped, creating a CONSTANT VOLUME.

This constant volume does not change. If it did, atoms would possess electrostatic charges. Hence, the volume of 3d space within this enclosed system remains the same no matter how fast the atom moves.

Because the radius of the atom is the length of one of the vortices, the radius of the atom now becomes a function of the maximum volume of space per unit of measured time that can flow from the electron to the proton, or from the proton to the electron without bunching up or backing up around either particle. (A situation which does not appear to happen, for if it did, its ACTUAL velocity would drop below the speed of light. Which doesn't happen. If it did, the electrostatic charges on protons and electrons would be variables instead of constants.)

Also, the fact that the electron and proton are of different sizes in no way effects our calculations. The same volume of space flowing out of one particle flows into the other.

The Formulas:
#1 The radius of the atom when motionless:

A hundred years ago, the results of the Michelson Morley experiment created havoc in the world of physics. In an effort to come up with an explanation, Lorentz and Fitzgerals, both working independently of each other, came up with the following proposal. Each man stated that one possible explanation for the unusual effect of seeing no difference in the travel times for the beams of light travelling between the two sets of mirrors set perpendicular and parallel to the direction of travel - would be the shrinkage of matter parallel to the direction of travel. If exactly the right amount of shrinkage occurs, the parallel beam which is moving slower than the perpendicular beam has less distance to travel, allowing it to arrive at the target at the same time as the perpendicular beam which is moving faster.

So how does matter shrink? Furthermore, why does it shrink by EXACTLY THE RIGHT AMOUNT to make it appear as if it never shrank at all?

To answer these questions, it must first determine what is happening when the atom is not moving. Then, it might be possible to determine what conditions are changing when the atom is moving.

To accomplish this task, we examine the internal workings of the hydrogen atom. As seen from the Vortex Theory, a hydrogen atom is made up of a 3d hole bent into higher dimensional space (the proton), a 3d hole bent out of higher dimensional space (The electron), and two flowing vortices of 3d space flowing between them. These two vortices flowing in opposite directions to each other create an ENCLOSED LOOP of circulating space. This enclosed loop contains a fixed volume of flowing space.

[Note: because the proton and the electron both possess the same electrostatic charge, *the same volume of 3d space is flowing into and out of each hole.* Therefore, even though the one particle is larger than the other, the cross sectional areas of the space flowing into and out of each particle are mathematically equal.]

The vortices, the particles, and the direction of their flows can be illustrated in the following drawing:

FIGURE A-1

Three Dimensional
Space (3d space)

Higher Dimensional
Space (Hd space)

Since the velocity into either particle equals the velocity out. And since the cross sectional area at any place on the length of either vortex *contains the same volume* of 3d space flowing through it, the volume of the flow into and out of each particle can be calculated in the following way:

$$\text{since:} \quad \textbf{Flow} = (\text{area})(\text{velocity})$$
$$\text{then:} \quad \textbf{Flow} = (ft^2)(ft/sec)$$

To further simplify all calculations, the radius of the hydrogen atom has been greatly enlarged to a value of ONE FOOT. The cross sectional area is ONE SQUARE FOOT. And the velocity of the vortex - the speed of light (C) - has been greatly reduced to ONE-FOOT PER SECOND.

(Also, because we are interested in how the atom shrinks at velocities approaching the speed of light, the path of the electron about the proton is irrelevant to our discussion. Only the position of the electron on the shell is important for our proof. How the electron reached that position does not effect our results.)

When the atom is NOT moving in relation to the BACKDROP OF SPACE, using the units in the above paragraph, the volume of space flowing INTO or OUT of either particle for any position of the electron on its shell is equal to:

$$\text{volume in} = (1\text{ft}^2)(1\text{ft/sec}) = 1\text{ft}^3/\text{sec}$$

$$\text{volume out} = (1\text{ft}^2)(1\text{ft/sec}) = 1\text{ft}^3/\text{sec}$$

$$\text{Consequently: Volume In} = \text{Volume Out} = 1\text{ft}^3/\text{sec}$$

For the purposes of our proof, the flow of 3d space into or out of either particle is equated to the constant value of ONE CUBIC FOOT PER SECOND. This constant represents the value of the electrostatic charge on either the electron or the proton in free space. Since these values are always measured the same no matter what the speed of the "reference frame" the particle is measured in, this value will always be a constant. Hence, the measured volume of space flowing into or out of a particle is always the same no matter what reference frame it is measured in. In other words, just as a traveler in the fast moving reference frame of a spaceship measures the speed of light as a constant value, he also measures the charges on the electrons and protons within his ship as constant values too.

#2 Factors effecting the volume of the flow:

Because the two vortices have created an entrapped circulating flow of CONSTANT VOLUME, changes in their lengths create changes in the cross sectional area of the flow. The change in the cross-sectional area of the flow creates changes in the volume of the flow. Therefore, to obtain the correct flow into or out of the electron or proton per unit of measured time the volume must be divided by the LENGTH of the vortices. Also, when the atom is not moving, because the length of the vortices are equal to "one" radius of the atom, the actual change in length is not as important as its percentage of length change.

The size of the atom is so incredibly small that changes in its length are meaningless to us - unless we have something to reference them to. Hence, by using a percentage of length change and then changing this value into a decimal, we do not have to know the actual microscopic value of the length change that occurs. Instead, we can say that the diameter of the atom shrank to 50% if its size, or to .5, (one half) of its original length. These are values we can easily relate to. Consequently, the length of the flow is divided by its unit of length to change it into a PERCENTAGE of the radius:

$$\text{FLOW} = \dfrac{(\text{Area})(\text{Velocity})}{\left[\dfrac{\text{length}}{\text{Unit of length}}\right]} = (1\text{ft}^2)(1\text{ft/sec}) = 1\text{ft}^3/\text{sec}$$

Note: even though "time dilation" will be discussed later, its effects are intertwined with length shrinkage and must be used here. This is necessary because the length of a *measured second* increases at high velocities. Consequently, a larger volume of space now flows per second of MEASURED time. Therefore, the volume must be multiplied by the amount a measured second increases at this high velocity:

$$\text{Flow} = \frac{(\text{Area})(\text{Velocity})}{\left[\dfrac{\text{length}}{\text{Unit of Length}}\right]} \cdot \frac{1}{\sqrt{1 - v^2/c^2}} = 1\,\text{ft}^3/\text{sec}$$

Note: these time dilation effects are equal to the slower apparent velocity of the round trip time of the two vortices and are not a function of "time". [see **table #3**]

[Note too: It should be reiterated that this book is not being written to dispute the "phenomenon of time" (which does exist as a real illusion). But rather, to show that time only exists as a function of velocity, and does not exist upon its own as a fundamental principle of the universe. Consequently, the use of time (as a stopwatch) in this formula is to MEASURE the distance between two events in exactly the same way as a yardstick measures the distance between two objects.]

To simplify our calculations, since the value of the cross sectional area of the vortex is multiplied by its velocity change when the atom is moving, this variable is designated the FLOWING VOLUME, in what can now be called the MAIN FORMULA:

FORMULA #1

$$\text{Flow} = \frac{(\text{Flowing Volume})}{\left[\dfrac{\text{length}}{1\text{ft}}\right]} \cdot \frac{1}{\sqrt{1 - v^2/c^2}} = 1\,\text{ft}^3/\text{sec}$$

Three important points of view

As was previously explained in *THE END OF THE CONCEPT OF "TIME" Book I*, that instead of just one vision of the universe (the relativistic vision) - there are actually three! Consequently, assuming this hydrogen atom is part of a spaceship, when the ship begins to move at velocity V, to understand why this atom, and the rest of the ship change shape, this hydrogen atom must be observed from all three different points of view:

A. The omnipresent point of view from higher dimensional space. [A Godlike view: seeing all, and knowing all.]

B. The point of view from a traveler inside the ship.

C. The point of view from inside the electron or the proton.

The Proof:

#1 When the atom moves at velocity "V"

When the space ship is not moving, when it is motionless in reference to the

backdrop of space, the three points of view previously defined are listed below:
FIGURE A-2

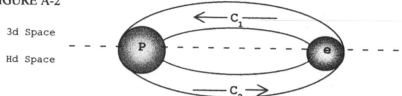

3d Space

Hd Space

Where: [C1 represents the speed of the three dimensional vortex]
[C2 represents the speed of the higher dimensional vortex]
(C represents the speed of light)

WHEN MOTIONLESS IN REFERENCE TO THE BACKDROP OF SPACE:
A. From the omnipresent point of view, all three of these values are equal:
$[C1 = C2 = C]$
B. From the traveler's point of view things are different. He cannot see either vortex, nor could he measure the round trip time if he could. The best he can do is measure the round trip time of light between mirrors (perform the Michelson Morley experiment within his spaceship). (And if he does, he finds the speed is still equal to "C", the speed of light.)
C. From the point of view within the electron or proton, all three of these values are equal: $[C1 = C2 = C]$

However, when the atom begins to move at velocity V, the situation changes dramatically:

WHEN THE ATOM MOVES AT VELOCITY V:
A. From the omnipresent point of view, the velocities of the two vortices are still equal: $C1 = C2$. Even though everything is moving, nothing, neither the proton, the electron, nor the flowing vortices are moving faster than the speed of light.
B. From the traveler's point of view within the spaceship, everything appears normal. The traveler cannot see what is happening within the atom. He can only make observations on what he can observe. So for him, everything still appears exactly as it was, nothing has changed.

Since it will be shown that length shrinks, and the measurement of time slows down, if he again performs the Michelson Morley experiment, nothing appears to be any different than before. The round trip of the light between the mirrors is still measured to be equal to "C", the speed of light.
C. But from **INSIDE** the electron or proton, the velocities of the two vortices now "**appear**" to be drastically different.
FIGURE A-3

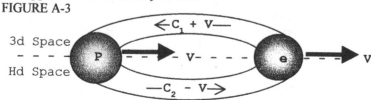

3d Space

Hd Space

```
HENCE:    VELOCITY INTO ELECTRON   = C - V
          VELOCITY OUT OF ELECTRON = C + V
```

The reason why the same set of circumstances creates three completely different points of view is explained in the following way:
A. From the omnipresent point of view, the actual speed of the vortices remains the same. Even though the two particles are now moving at velocity "V", **NOTHING IN THIS SYSTEM IS MOVING FASTER THAN THE SPEED OF LIGHT!**
For example: if an imaginary mark could be placed upon the space flowing out of the electron, it would reach the proton quicker, not because it was flowing faster, but rather, because the proton is moving towards it. Even though such a mark arrives at the proton faster than it would if the atom was not moving, the actual velocity of the vortex has not changed: **IT IS STILL FLOWING AT THE SPEED OF LIGHT, "C".**
The opposite is true for a mark placed upon the space flowing out of the proton. Since the electron is moving away from this mark, as this mark moves towards the electron, it now takes longer to arrive at the electron than it would if the atom was not moving. Even so, it must always be remembered that the vortex is **STILL FLOWING AT THE SPEED OF LIGHT, "C".**
B. From the traveler's point of view within the spaceship, nothing has changed. Again, since it will be shown that the length of the ship parallel to the direction of travel shrinks, and a measured second slows down, when the traveler again measures the time it takes for the light to travel between the two sets of mirrors he has set up to perform the Michelson Morley experiment, he still sees no difference. The result he views is the same we view here upon the earth: unless he looks out a window, it appears as if the spaceship is not moving at all.
C. **HOWEVER**, from the point of view within the electron (or proton), things have changed radically. From this viewpoint, the electron is not moving. Consequently, the space flowing into the electron now appears to be entering at the **APPARENT VELOCITY** of C-V, and exiting at the **APPARENT VELOCITY** of C+V! (The opposite is true for a viewpoint within the proton.)
And again, it is extremely important to understand that when the atom is moving, **NOTHING, NO PART OF THE ATOM OR ITS VORTICES ARE MOVING FASTER THAN THE SPEED OF LIGHT.** The vortices are still flowing at the speed of light. However, because the positions of the two particles are constantly changing, from the viewpoints **within** the electron and the proton, the velocities of the two vortices are now entering and exiting the particles at different apparent velocities. Hence, the volume of space flowing into a particle no longer equals the volume flowing out of a particle. If nothing changed, an impossible situation would develop where the flow out of a particle would exceed the flow into it. It would be analogous to having a valve where one gallon per second flowed in, and five gallons per second flowed out.
The only way for flowing space to avoid this disparity, is to have some of the

volume from the faster flow add to the volume of the slower flow, then, the volume into and out of each particle remains equal. The calculation of this value has been dubbed - THE FLOWING VOLUME.

#2 The flowing volume parallel to the velocity of travel:
When the electron and the proton are in the positions seen in figure 2-1 making them parallel to the hydrogen atom's velocity of travel, (and moving from left to right across the page), the calculation of the FLOWING VOLUME has a very simple solution:

WHERE V = .866C

Apparent Velocity into electron:
  (1ft/sec) - (.866ft/sec) = .134ft/sec

Apparent Velocity out of electron:
  (1ft/sec) + (.866ft/sec) = 1.866ft/sec

To find the FLOWING VOLUME, the following identity is used:

VOLUME IN = VOLUME OUT

or,

FORMULA #2

(VELOCITY IN)(AREA) = (VELOCITY OUT)(AREA)

For V = .866C:
  (Velocity In)(Area) = (Velocity Out)(Area)

$$(.134 \text{ft/sec})(1 \text{ft}^2 + X \text{ft}^2) = (1.866 \text{ft/sec})(1 \text{ft}^2 - X \text{ft}^2)$$

$$X = .866$$

$$(.134 \text{ft/sec})(1 \text{ft}^2 + .866 \text{ft}^2) = (1.866 \text{ft/sec})(1 \text{ft}^2 - .866 \text{ft}^2)$$
$$.250 \text{ft}^3/\text{sec} = .250 \text{ft}^3/\text{sec}$$

Cross sectional views of the vortices at .866c :

FIGURE A-4

C + V   cross sectional area = .134ft^2

Cross sectional area = 1.87ft^2

C–V

Note how the cross sectional area of the flow travelling at the apparent velocity of 1.866c is now about 14 times less than the cross sectional area of the flow travelling at the apparent velocity of .134c.

Hence, the volumes of the two flows into and out of each particle are again equal:

$$.250ft^3/sec = .250ft^3/sec$$

However, the above identity is incorrect, because when V = .866c, one second of measured "time" no longer equals one second of measured "time" when motionless. To compensate for this discrepancy, the measurement of time needs to be adjusted with the following formula: [The formula developed by Lorentz]

$$dt' = \frac{dt}{\sqrt{1 - v^2/c^2}} = \text{TIME DILATION EFFECTS}$$

Where: dt equals the measured change in time occurring in a motionless frame of reference.

Dt' equals the measured change in time occurring in a moving frame of reference divided by the square root of 1 minus the value of the square of the velocity divided by the square of the speed of light.

(Note: although this formula will be discussed later, it must be used now in our calculations in order for us to proceed.)

Therefore: the flow of .250 cubic feet per second in our time frame must be changed to account for the time dilation effects which occur in this faster moving time frame:

$$(.250ft^3/sec) . \frac{1}{\sqrt{1 - (.866)^2}} = .500ft^3/sec$$

However, this flow still does not equal the "one cubic foot per second" flow of space which takes place in the vortices when the atom is not moving. More flowing space from the vortices needs to flow into the proton and the electron. This discrepancy causes the flow to shorten its length to increase the volume of the flow.

Hence, the electron must move closer to the proton to again make the volume of the flow return to its constant value of "one cubic foot per second".

And it just so happens, *that the new shorter length necessary to again return the flow to "one cubic foot per second", is EXACTLY THE SAME LENGTH THE ATOM SHRINKS AS PREDICTED BY LORENTZ AND FITZGERALDS (EVEN THOUGH THEY DIDN'T KNOW WHY)!!!*

Since: $(ft) \sqrt{1 - v^2/c^2} = (ft)[1 - (.866)^2]^{\frac{1}{2}} = .500ft$

Then: $\dfrac{.500ft^3/sec}{\dfrac{.500ft}{1ft}} = 1FT^3/SEC \ !\ !\ !$

#3 The flowing volume perpendicular to the direction of travel:

The atom does not shrink in the direction perpendicular to the velocity of travel, because it does not have to.

Unlike the direction parallel to the velocity of travel, in the direction perpendicular to the velocity of travel, both flowing volumes have IDENTICAL APPARENT VELOCITIES, making their cross sectional areas equal. Consequently, one flow does not have to subtract from itself to add to the other.

Furthermore, unlike its non-moving condition, the two vortices cannot flow directly towards each particle. When flowing space is discharged from a moving particle towards another particle perpendicular to it, space cannot flow directly towards it. If it did, its resultant vector "R", would be moving faster than the speed of light "C":

FIGURE A-5

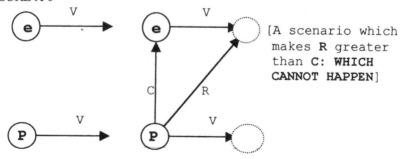

[A scenario which makes **R** greater than **C**: **WHICH CANNOT HAPPEN**]

Therefore, when space travelling at the speed of light flows out of one particle towards the other, which is above or below it, it now has to travel at the apparent velocity of the "y" vector:

FIGURE A-6

WHERE: C = SPEED OF LIGHT
V = %C = V/C
Y = %C = Y/C

In this situation, with both particles directly perpendicular to each other, "y" equals the APPARENT VELOCITY of the space both flowing from the electron to the proton and from the proton to the electron. Because the angles between the "V" vectors and the "C" vectors are the same, both "y" vectors are also equal to each other via similar triangles.

To calculate the value of "y" when v = .866c, the Pythagorean theorem is used:

$$C^2 = V^2 + y^2$$

$$y^2 = C^2 - V^2$$

$$y^2 = 1 - (.866)^2$$

$$y = .5 \text{ft/sec}$$

Hence: APPARENT VELOCITY into the electron = .5ft/sec
APPARENT VELOCITY out of the electron = .5ft/sec

To calculate the value of the FLOWING VOLUME Formula #2 is used:

Formula #2:   (Vel. In)(Area) = (Vel. Out)(Area)

$$(.5\text{ft/sec})(1\text{ft}^2 + X\text{ft}^2) = (.5\text{ft/sec})(1\text{ft}^2 - X\text{ft}^2)$$

$$(X)(1\text{ft}^3/\text{sec}) = 0$$

$$X = 0$$

$$(.5\text{ft/sec})(1\text{ft}^2) = (.5\text{ft/sec})(1\text{ft}^2)$$

$$.5\text{ft}^3/\text{sec} = .5\text{ft}^3/\text{sec}$$

To calculate the LENGTH of the flow, Formula #1 is used:

Formula #1: $\text{(Flowing Volume)} \cdot \dfrac{1}{\sqrt{1 - v^2/c^2}} = 1\text{ft}^3/\text{sec}$

where the Flowing Volume is divided by $\left[\dfrac{\text{Length}}{\text{Unit of Length}}\right]$

Given: $\dfrac{(.5\text{ft}^3/\text{sec })}{\left[\dfrac{\text{Length}}{1\text{ft}}\right]} \cdot \dfrac{1}{\sqrt{1 - (.866)^2}} = 1\text{ft}^3/\text{sec}$

Since: $\dfrac{1\text{ft}^3/\text{sec}}{\left[\dfrac{\text{Length}}{1\text{ft}}\right]} = 1\text{ft}^3/\text{sec}$

Then: Length = *1ft !!!*

Consequently, in the direction perpendicular to the velocity of travel, THE RADIUS OF THE ATOM DOES NOT SHRINK! HENCE, THE DIAMETER DOES NOT SHRINK EITHER: JUST AS PREDICTED BY LORENTZ AND FITZGERALDS (EVEN THOUGH THEY DIDN'T KNOW WHY)!!!

#4 The radius of the atom from 0 to 90 degrees:

The key to discovering the shape of the atom from 0 to 90 degrees is found in the changing lengths of its radius. And the key to discovering the lengths of its changing radius is found in the changing values of the APPARENT VELOCITIES of the two vortices as they rotate with the electron about the proton.

Because it is impossible (at this writing) to tell what path the electron is following about the proton in a hydrogen atom, only the electron's positions at different places on the shell it forms around the proton can be described. (Note, as was said before, for the purposes of our discussion, how the electron got to a certain position on the shell it forms about the proton is not as important as the radius of the atom at that position.)

Therefore, the following calculations are only for various positions of the electron on its shell, and for the appropriate radii of the hydrogen atom at these locations.

To calculate the APPARENT VELOCITIES of the vortices in the region greater than 0 degrees yet less than 90 degrees, the viewpoints of the omnipresent observer, and the traveler within the spaceship must be re-examined.

By now it should be apparent that the travelers viewpoint within the spaceship is also our viewpoint, our earthly viewpoint as seen from the "spaceship earth".

From this viewpoint we can only see what we can see. And the sight we see is one of "normality". Every day, everything appears normal to us.

This viewpoint is also limited to a certain degree. We cannot look into the atom and measure the velocities of the vortices. Indeed, we cannot even see these vortices, we can only perceive them with our imaginations.

However, if we could see our world from the viewpoint of the omnipresent observer, we would see a totally different vision of reality. Nothing would seem "normal" to us, especially the flows of the vortices.

For example, when the electron and proton align to form a $90°$ with the direction of travel, from the travelers perspective it appears that both vortices are travelling at the speed of light.

FIGURE A-7

However, as seen from the omnipresent point of view, for a $90°$ angle the vortices are actually flowing at the slower apparent velocity of the "y" vector:

FIGURE A-8

WHERE: C = SPEED OF LIGHT
V = %C = V/C
Y = %C = Y/C

To understand why this phenomenon is taking place, it is important to reiterate that the traveler is viewing an illusion, while the omnipresent observer is viewing reality.

The traveler views his surroundings as if everything is sitting dead still, while the omnipresent observer sees the world (or spaceship) in motion. Hence the omnipresent observer sees what is really happening. He sees the atom moving through space at velocity (V) causing space to flow at the slower apparent velocity of the "y" vector.

The reason why the omnipresent observer sees the space flowing at this slower apparent velocity is again due to the fact that while moving at velocity (V), the vortex flowing FROM the proton TO the electron cannot flow directly towards it at the speed of light. As previously mentioned, if it did, its resultant vector would exceed the speed of light. Hence, to account for this fact the following formula is used:

FORMULA #3 $[(\text{Cos A})(Z_1) + V]^2 + [(\text{Sin A})(Z_1)]^2 = C^2$

This formula is merely an extension of the Pythagorean Theorem with "$[(\text{Cos A})(Z_1) + V]^2$" representing the horizontal component, while the value of "$[(\text{Sin A})(Z_1)]^2$" represents the vertical component. The value of "Z" is the apparent velocity, while "C" is the speed of light.

Since there are two vortices, formula #3 is the formula for what will be called the UP VORTEX. The UP VORTEX flows against the direction of travel. The UP VORTEX flows through higher dimensional space from the proton to the electron in Quadrants #1 and #4 of the Cartesian Co-ordinate system when the atom is moving from left to right across the page.

The vector which flows through three-dimensional space from the electron to the proton in Quadrants #1 and #4 is designated the BACK VORTEX.

The value of the BACK VORTEX is found by the following formula:

FORMULA #4 $[(\text{Cos A})(Z_2) - V]^2 + [(\text{Sin A})(Z_2)]^2 = C^2$

As before, this formula is also merely an extension of the Pythagorean Theorem. The only difference between this formula and formula #3 is the value of "V". Here, velocity "V" has a negative value. This condition arises because the vortex is flowing backwards towards the particle which is moving forward towards it. Making it appear as if this vortex is moving faster. However, it, like the UP VORTEX is always flowing at "C", the speed of light. In reference to the "backdrop of space" this speed never changes, no matter how fast the atom is moving.

The study of these two formulas shows that they also contain the solutions to the two problems we have already solved: the direction PARALLEL to the velocity of travel, and the direction PERPENDICULAR to the velocity of travel:

[When angle A equals 0 degrees, the sine equals 0 while the cosine equals 1; making "Z_1", the apparent velocity, of the UP VORTEX equal to C - V, and "Z_2", the apparent velocity of the BACK VORTEX equal to C + V: allowing us to find the length of the atom in the direction PARALLEL to the velocity of travel.

Conversely, when angle A equals 90 degrees, the Sine equals 1, while the Cosine now equals 0. This makes "Z", the apparent velocity of both the UP and BACK VORTICES equal to the square root of C squared minus V squared: allowing us to find the length of the atom in the direction PERPENDICULAR to the direction of travel.

Note too, that when the atom is not moving, "V" equals 0, making the value of "Z" equal to "C", the speed of light.

To solve for the value of "Z" in either formula, the following formula is used:

FORMULA #5

$$Z_{1&2} = [(-V)(Cos\ A)] \pm \sqrt{(V^2)(Cos\ A)^2 - V^2 + C^2}$$

Note, the addition of the two terms in this equation gives us the value of the apparent velocity for the UP VORTEX, while their subtraction equals the value of the BACK VORTEX. (The difference in their signs indicates they are traveling in opposite directions.)

Also, as was previously mentioned, formulas #3 and #4 are for the positions of the electron and proton when they are in Quadrants #1 and #4 of the Cartesian Co-ordinate system, while quadrants #2 and #3 use the same formulas with their positions reversed: formula #3 is for the BACK vortex, while formula #4 is for the UP vortex.

Putting all of this together, once we have found the values of the APPARENT VELOCITY UP and the APPARENT VELOCITY BACK, we can then substitute these values into formula #2 and find the value of the FLOWING VOLUME. The value of the flowing volume is then substituted back into the MAIN FORMULA to find the value of the LENGTH OF THE FLOW: which equals the radius of the hydrogen atom at this particular location of the electron on the shell.

FOR EXAMPLE: When the atom is moving at a velocity of .866C, to find the radius of the atom where it makes a 45 degree angle to the direction of the velocity of travel, the following procedure is used:

Step #1 Find the values of the apparent velocities of the Up and Back vortices:

Formula #5

$$Z_{1&2} = [(-V)(Cos\ A)] \pm \sqrt{(V^2)(Cos\ A)^2 - V^2 + C^2}$$

$$Z_{1&2} = [(-.866)(.707)] \pm \sqrt{(.866)^2(.707)^2 - (.866)^2 + (1)^2}$$

$$Z_{1&2} = [-.612] \pm [.790]$$

$$UP = [-.612] + [.790] = .178\ ft/sec$$

$$Back = [-.612] - [.790] = 1.402\ ft/sec$$

[Note, the negative sign is not necessary for our solution.]

Step #2 Find the value of the flowing volume:

Formula #2 (Vel. In)(Area) = (Vel. Out)(Area)

Since: Velocity Up = Velocity In
And: Velocity Back = Velocity Out
Then: (Velocity Up)(Area) = (Velocity Back)(Area)
So: $(.178ft/sec)(1ft^2 + Xft^2) = (1.402ft/sec)(1ft^2 - Xft^2)$
$$X = .775$$

Hence: Flowing Volume $= (.178ft/sec)(1ft^2 + .775ft^2) = 0.316ft^3/sec$

Step #3 To find the length of the radius at 45 degrees to the direction of the velocity of travel:

```
Formula #1
Flow = (Flowing Volume) .      1         = 1ft³/sec
        ⎡Length⎤           √ 1 - V²/C²
        ⎣(1ft)_⎦
```

```
Flow = (.316ft³/sec) .        1          = 1ft³/sec
        ⎡Length⎤         √ 1 - (.866)²
        ⎣(1ft) _⎦
```

```
     Length = .63ft
```

Hence, when the positions of the electron and the proton are such that a line drawn between them forms an angle of 45 degrees to the direction of the velocity of travel, the radius shrinks to a value of .63 ft.

Plotting a number of angles with their corresponding radii yields the following table:

TABLE #1

	Angle	Radius
	0	.500
[Note: these values are for	5	.502
all four regions of the	10	.506
Cartesian co-ordinate system.	15	.513
for the (+X, +Y)Region;	20	.524
the (+X, -Y)Region; the	25	.538
the (-X, +Y)Region; and	30	.55
Region; and the (-X, -Y)	35	.58
Region.	40	.60
When plotted, they create	45	.63
a cross section of the	50	.67
hydrogen atom, and when	55	.71
this cross section is	60	.76
rotated about the X axis,	65	.81
its complete three	70	.86
dimensional shape	75	.91
is created.]	80	.96
	85	.99
	90	1.00

WHEN THE VALUES FROM TABLE #2 ARE PLOTTED UPON GRAPH
PAPER, A SPECTACULAR ELLIPTICAL SHAPE COMES INTO VIEW:

FIGURE A-9

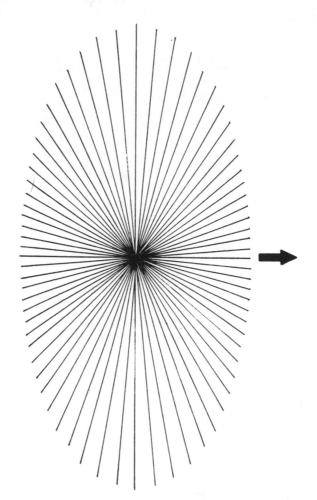

#5 The phenomenon of time:
  The speed of light is the first clue to deducing the true nature of time.
  The true nature of time is discovered by first realizing that the speed of light is
not a variable. It is one of the great constants of nature. In free space, all photons
of light move at the same speed; this extremely important piece of knowledge
allows us to determine exactly how the phenomenon of time is created.
  Although there appears to be a number of ways to create photons, one way is
within the vortex. In the vortex theory, it was proposed that a photon of light is a

condensed packet of 3d space thrown from the flowing vortex joining the particles of an atom together. Because the speed of light is not a variable, all photons appear to move at the same rate everywhere; an inference that allows us to hypothesize that the speed of all of the vortices in all of the atoms in the universe are also flowing at the same rate. A stunning realization that allows us to arrive at the equally astounding conclusion – **that the phenomenon of time is created by the speed of the vortex!**

This simply remarkable conclusion, results from the fact that all motions in the universe begin with, and are functions of, the speed of the vortex as mentioned in this book. For example, because the electron is nothing more than a hole in space through which the vortex is flowing, the velocity of the space flowing through it governs the speed of the electron about the proton. The maxim speed the atom can move is also function of the space flowing in the vortex. The velocity of the atom cannot exceed the speed of the vortex. If it did, the vortex flowing in the direction of travel could never catch up to the particle it was trying to reach. Hence, the speed of light is the terminal velocity for the matter of the universe.

Then there are the "after effects" of the speed of the vortex.

The speed of the reconfiguration of space around particles is also limited. Since the space surrounding a particle is pulled into or pushed out of it at the speed of the vortex, as the particle moves, it reconfigures itself around the particle at the speed of the vortex.

The forces of nature also reconfigure themselves at the speed of the vortex. Each force is a manifestation of the *dense and flowing space* created by the holes we once thought were particles. Consequently, each force is also unable to reconfigure itself faster than the speed of the vortex.

To sum it all up, because every motion of matter, space, energy, and the forces of nature are a function of the velocity of the vortices, the motion of everything in the universe is a function of the vortices. Hence, every synchronistic motion that is responsible for creating the phenomenon of time can be traced to the velocity of the vortices.

The phenomenon of time is the result of all the harmonic and sequential atomic, chemical, biological, and astronomical motions creating an orderly sequence of constantly repeating events. These constantly repeating events create a sense of order and harmony in the universe. This order and harmony is responsible for the creation of the phenomenon of time.

However, although the phenomenon of time is real, time isn't. The order and harmony of the constantly repeating events in the universe are not being created by "time" they are created by the velocity of the space flowing in the vortices.

It should be mentioned that the velocity of the space flowing within the vortices is theorized to be a function of the elasticity of space itself! (A theory that will be proposed in the next book of this three part series.)

Because I was once told by a professor of physics that space would have to be very dense to allow light to travel at the incredible speed that it does, and therefore could not bend or flow - this erroneous deduction must be dispelled. It is also necessary to dispel the equally wrong inference that the elasticity of space might itself be a function of time, and that time might still exist.

The way I like to dispel these wrong ideas is to mention an incredible fact that surfaced during the course of these investigations: I like to call it – HOW FAST IS FAST!

This incredible discovery stems from the fact that the speed of light might not be very fast at all! Light might not be moving at 186,000 miles a second! In fact, how fast it is really moving is unknown and can never be measured!

This amazing discovery came from the deduction that every motion in the universe used as a reference to compare other motions to is a function of the speed of the vortices! All other motions are created by the speed of the vortices. The vortices might very well be flowing at the speed of foot per second, or a billion miles per second and we would never know it!

All we can say is this, "That according to the "backdrop of space", the vortices are moving." We can use the backdrop of space to compare motions to, and we can compare the speed of one motion to another. We can state that one motion is faster than another, - but we cannot tell exactly how fast those motions are! So "how fast is fast", nobody knows!

#6 Time dilation:

Because *dense and flowing space* moves at the same rate everywhere, all similar motions take place at a fixed rate everywhere. Accordingly, if a situation develops in some area of the universe where *dense and flowing space* can no longer move at its maximum rate, motions in this area will slow down, creating greater distances between the repetition of events occurring here, and the repetition of similar events occurring elsewhere. Such a situation would make it appear as if "time" has somehow slowed down.

Which is precisely what happens at near light velocities.

At near light velocities, the SLOWER APPARENT VELOCITY of *dense and flowing space* causes all motions to slow down, creating the phenomenon of "time dilation".

FOR EXAMPLE:

When the atom is moving at $V = .866c$, if the length of the radius of the atom, at any point on its shell, is first divided by the apparent velocity of the space flowing "up" and then divided by the apparent velocity of the space flowing "back", a wonderful discovery is made. We find that the sum of these two different times now equals a measured value for the round trip time which is *twice* that for when the atom was not moving relative to the backdrop of space.

In other words, when the hydrogen atom is moving at .866c, it now takes twice as long for flowing space to make the round trip between the electron and the proton than it did when the atom was not moving. This phenomenon is demonstrated in the following table:

Angle "A"	Length of radius	Apparent Velocity UP	Apparent Velocity BACK	Time up	Time back	Total time
		TABLE #3				
		[For V = .866C]				
90 Deg	1.0 ft	.5 ft/sec	.5 ft/sec	2 sec	2 sec	4 sec
80	.958	.3718	.6724	2.575	1.424	4.00
70	.860	.2849	.8773	3.019	.980	4.00
60	.756	.2284	1.0944	3.310	.690	4.00
50	.668	.1916	1.305	2.486	.512	4.00
40	.602	.1673	1.494	3.597	.403	4.00
30	.555	.1514	1.6514	3.664	.336	4.00
20	.523	.1410	1.769	3.709	.296	4.00
10	.506	.1358	1.8414	3.725	.275	4.00
0	.500	.1340	1.8660	3.730	.270	4.00

Note: In the TOTAL TIME column, the addition of the TIME UP and the TIME BACK columns were rounded off to 4.0 seconds.

Because only three significant figures are used in the above table, the TIME UP and the TIME BACK do not appear to add up to the value of 4.0 seconds. This discrepancy occurs because only values of many, many significant figures add up to 4.0 seconds. Therefore, this liberty was taken to conserve space. Note too, when the atom is NOT moving, the value of the TIME UP and the TIME BACK are equal to "1" second each way: which total "2" seconds for a round trip.

For a velocity of .866C, notice how the total round trip time of 4.0 seconds is always twice as long as the previous round trip time of 2.0 seconds when the atom was not moving.

When the round trip times for many different velocities are calculated, the difference between their round trip time and the "at rest" round trip time is always equal to:

CONTEMPORARY VIEW:

$$dt' = \frac{dt}{\sqrt{1 - v^2/c^2}} = \text{TIME DILATION EFFECTS}$$

Where dt' equals the difference in a measured second of time in the moving frame of reference which is travelling at velocity "V", and the measured second of time (dt) in the non-moving frame of reference.

When moving at .866C, ANY MOTION made by matter now takes twice as long as it did when it was at rest in reference to the backdrop of space.

VORTEX THEORY:

$$d(space)' = \frac{d(space)}{\sqrt{1 - V^2 / C^2}} = \text{TIME DILATION EFFECTS}$$

Where d(space)' equals the apparent elasticity of space in a moving frame of reference which is traveling at velocity "V", and d(space) equals the elasticity of space in the non-moving frame of reference.

#7 The explanation of the Michelson Morley Experiment

The explanation of the Michelson Morley experiment is now apparent. When moving at any velocity, because of the way the atoms are constructed out of *dense and flowing space*, the lengths of physical objects ACTUALLY SHRINK in the direction parallel to the velocity of motion, and the SLOWER APPARENT VELOCITY of space causes all motions to slow proportionally. Hence, the measurement of the speed of light is the same for any and all velocities an individual happens to be travelling at.

In this paper, the proof of the length shrinkage and time dilation effects used one set of vortices in one hydrogen atom. Even though this was a simplification, because all protons and all electrons in all atoms will be connected in a similar way, all of the other atoms in all of the other elements will behave like those described here. Causing their lengths parallel to the direction of velocity to shrink, while their lengths perpendicular to the velocity of travel maintain the same dimensions.

Furthermore, since every set of vortices in all of the other atoms of everything in the Earth slow down according to the slower apparent velocity of *dense and flowing space*, the motions of everything slows accordingly: creating time dilation effects.

Hence we now have a third explanation for the Michelson Morley experiment. Because the lengths of everything in the Earth including Michelson and Morley's apparatus shrink parallel to the direction of the Earth's velocity, and since the lengths of everything in the Earth perpendicular to the Earth's velocity do not shrink, the travel times between the two sets of mirrors is always the same.

Also, since the slower apparent velocity makes all of the motions of everything in the Earth slow proportionally, no change was seen during the different seasons of the year as the Earth speeds up or slows down slightly during its orbit of the Sun.

When Michelson and Morley conducted their famous experiment, even though they made the lengths between their mirrors equal, and arranged them at 90 degree angles to each other, neither of these criterion are important.

The Michelson Morley experiment measures the relative time difference between the two sets of mirrors. Hence, the relative time difference for any two sets of mirrors set at different lengths from each other, or at angles other than 90 degrees will always show the same relative time difference no matter how they are rotated to each other, to the direction of travel, or what velocity they move at.

This effect occurs because the radii of atoms at different angles to the velocity of travel all have different lengths and different apparent velocities. This creates round trip travel times equal to the round trip travel times of all other radii at all other angles to the velocity of travel (as demonstrated in table #1).

Consequently, if the distance between one set of mirrors is one foot, and the distance between the other set is three feet, it will always take three times as long for light to travel between one set verses the other. Hence their relative travel times will always show this same difference no matter how they are positioned to the velocity of travel, or what the angle is between them.

End of proof

SOLVING FOR "Z", THE APPARENT VELOCITY, IN FORMULAS #3 AND #4:

Note: Although I am the originator of equations #3 and #4, the solution for the value of "Z" was derived by a young graduate student in Physics working on his PHD at *FLORIDA ATLANTIC UNIVERSITY* in Boca Raton Florida. To solve for "Z", the Quadratic Formula is used; Knowing this clue, the proof becomes so simple, a high school student can do it.

Ch24 THE SECRET OF TIME IS FINALLY EXPLAINED!

The human race has lived with the concept of time for at least five thousand years. But until now, nobody has known what it is or how it is created. However, that is all changed.

Here, at long last, is the explanation of how "time" – or rather the phenomenon of time is created:

Although "time" does not exist as a fundamental principle of the universe, the phenomenon of time is created by a hierarchy of speeds that begins with the velocity of the space flowing into and out of the three-dimensional holes of "matter".

Because it is easier to see this relationship when looking at the two vortices of the three-dimensional space flowing back and forth between the proton and the electron in the hydrogen atom, this example is used.

Earlier, it was shown how the speed of a photon of light is a function of the speed of the vortices. But here it must be stated that even this velocity is a function of something else!

The velocity of the space flowing within the vortices appears to be a result of the fastest speed that higher dimensional space is capable of bending and flexing.

This speed appears to be the fastest motion in the universe. Why the vortex possesses this speed will be examined in greater depth in book two of this three-part trilogy. For now, it can be said that this speed can be identified as the speed of light.

The speed of light is at the top or peak of a pyramid of speeds. Although the speed of light is the reference to which all other speeds are referred, the speed of light itself is a function of the velocity of the space flowing within the vortices.

The speed of the electron as it moves about the photon is also a function of the speed of the vortices. Since the electron is a hole created within three-dimensional space by the flow of one of the vortices, its position is determined by the changing position of the vortex. Hence its speed as it moves about the proton is a percentage of the speed of the vortices.

Since the proton is also a hole in space which three-dimensional space is flowing into, it cannot move faster than the speed of the space flowing into it. Hence its speed is also a function of the speed of the space in the vortices. The same is true for the three-dimensional space circulating within the neutron.

Since all atoms are made up of protons, electrons, and neutrons, the speed of the motions of all atoms is again a percentage of the speed of the vortices. The same holds true for molecules.

Since all molecules are made up of atoms, the speeds and the motions of all molecules are percentages of the speed of the atoms out of which they are made. Hence, a molecule's speed is also a function of the speed of the vortices as well.

And last but not least, at the very end of the hierarchy of motion, is the motion of planets, stars, and Galaxies. Because all planets, stars, and galaxies are made out of atoms and molecules, their much slower motions are also functions of the velocity of the space flowing within the vortices. (Note: the above is also true for antimatter atoms and molecules made up of anti-protons, positrons, and anti-neutrons.) This hierarchy of motions now allow the phenomenon of time to be explained.

Since all motions associated with the passage of time (including those created within clocks) are created either by light, or by the motions of matter, it is now easy to see that all of these motions are also functions of, and percentages of the speed of the space flowing within the vortices. Because all the vortices of all the atoms in the universe are flowing at the same rate, the same motions within every atom of every similar element and molecule throughout the universe also takes place at the same rate.

It should be noted here that if the vortices were flowing at different speeds at different places in the universe, the speed of the photons of light thrown from these vortices would be variables instead of constants. This would make the light coming from distant suns and galaxies travel at different speeds. Since this is not seen, the speeds of all the vortices are the same throughout the universe.

[And as will be seen in the second book of this three-part trilogy, this deduction gives us a clue as to how the universe was created.])

These similar motions are responsible for the creation of similar harmonic motions occurring everywhere at the same rate. These similar atomic, chemical, biological, and astronomical motions, no matter where they occur in the universe, create an orderly sequence of constantly repeating events. These constantly repeating events create order and harmony in the universe. This order and harmony is responsible for the creation of the phenomenon of time.

It can now be understood that all similar motions occur everywhere at the same rate not because of some metaphysical quality called "time", but simply because the *dense and flowing space* out of which everything in the universe is made moves at the same rate everywhere!

Because it could also be misconstrued that time does indeed exist and is in fact controlling how fast space can bend and flow, this mistaken idea must be dispelled. Realizing that the "bend-ability" of space is a function of its elastic properties dispels this idea. This "bend-ability" is an important subject because it relates to the "solid-ness" of space.

The topic of the "solid-ness" of space came up when I was once told by a professor of physics that space could not be made of anything because it would have to be extremely dense to allow light to move through it so fast. Consequently, if it was very dense it could not flow – making all of the ideas about *dense and flowing space* false. However, this type of reasoning is incorrect.

The speed of light is a function of the velocity of the vortex. Consequently, because we measure the speed of light with harmonic motions that are also functions of the speed of the vortex – there is no *motion in the universe that is independent of the speed of the vortex.* Therefore, any attempt to measure the speed of the vortex has to be done with another motion that is a function of the speed of the same vortex we are trying to measure. Hence, if the vortex moves slower, the velocity of the motion used to measure it also moves slower.

This deduction leads us to another astounding conclusion: the speed of the vortex could really be one foot per second, or one inch per second, or one millionth of an inch per second and we would never know it!

Because of this amazing fact, the length of a second – which seems very short to us, might really be very long! In fact, every motion in the universe might be so slow that it could have taken me a year to write this one sentence! Then again, a second might really be incredibly short. It is possible that it could have only taken a microsecond to write this entire book! Either way, we would never know it! We will never know it because no matter how fast or slow the vortices are moving, it will always appear to us and our instruments that they are moving at 186,000 miles per second – the speed of light! A simply astounding conclusion!

Ch25 TIME DILATION IS FINALLY EXPLAINED

Perhaps the most fascinating phenomenon that exists in the universe today is "Time Dilation".

When an object begins to move faster, from the 20th Century scientific view, its relationship with "time" somehow slows down. This is a real effect possessing astonishing results. The most famous of these effects is the "Twins Paradox":

Say for example when two twin boys were about eighteen years old, one of them left the earth for a long voyage on a spaceship to a distant star. This spaceship, traveling at .866C, which is nearly the speed of light (note, .25C is one-fourth the speed of light, .5C is one-half the speed of light, and .75C is three-fourths the speed of light. "C" stands for light speed.), reached the distant star and immediately turned around and came home.

Because the entire round trip took forty years, when the spaceship returned to earth, the brother who was now sixty-years old was there to meet him. However, when the spacecraft door opened, instead of him greeting another sixty year old man, he was amazed to find that his brother had only aged twenty years!

Even though the earthly calendar indicated he was gone for forty years, the calendar on the ship indicated he had been away for only twenty years! Amazed, they both realized that somehow, some kind of "time dilation" effect had occurred. Yet neither could explain how it happened.

Neither could anyone else in the world explain how it happened - that is until now! Here is how it happened.

When the spaceship left the earth, and begins to travel at a near light velocity, the atoms the ship is made of were moving at a much faster velocity than the atoms the earth is made of.

This means the electrons, protons, and neutrons of every atom within the ship are moving faster too. And again, just like before, *even though the vortices connecting every proton and electron continue to flow at precisely the speed of light, from the point of view within a proton, electron or neutron,* the speeds of the vortices appear to change. One vortex appears to be going much faster than the speed of light while the other appears to be going much slower!

The addition of these two speeds creates a slower round trip time for the space circulating within the vortices. Making the round trip take longer. Making the same round trip take place at what can be called, "THE SLOWER APPARENT VELOCITY." [Note: the same effect occurs for the space circulating within the neutron.]

Also, because the spaceship is moving, space is constantly reconfiguring itself around every tiny three-dimensional hole the ship is made of. As each individual hole moves, the space surrounding it is first bent towards it, and then away from it as it passes by. So even though a proton, electron, or neutron may not be attached to an atom, the space surrounding it ends up moving in two opposite directions, making it reconfigure around the particle at the rate of the slower apparent velocity too. Furthermore, because everything in the universe is constructed out of *dense and flowing space*, including energy, and the "forces of nature", all of their motions, and all of their interrelated motions, will also slow. In fact, the mathematics show that all of their motions will slow down exactly, and proportionally to the correspondingly slower apparent velocity of space when they are travelling in the faster moving frame of reference.

For simplicity sake, the spacecraft was said to be moving at a velocity of .866 the speed of light. This speed was chosen because at this velocity, the round-trip time of the vortices of every atom within the ship doubles. And when the round trip time doubles, and the reconfiguration of *dense and flowing space* doubles, every motion of every atom within the ship also doubles. Because of the hierarchy of motions described before, when the motions of atoms double, the motions of the objects made out of them double too. Making every motion take *twice as long* to complete.

Consequently, when the ship was sitting upon the earth, if it took one second to throw a baseball from one man to another within the ship, when moving at .866C it now takes twice as long. Hence, the ball itself now moves at a slower velocity that is directly proportional to the SLOWER APPARENT VELOCITY of the atoms it is constructed out of.

Also, since the atoms in the man's arm are now moving at the slower apparent velocity of space, it cannot move as fast as it could when the ship was motionless. Therefore, the man cannot throw the ball as fast as he could when the spaceship was not moving. However, since the motions of every atom in the ship have slowed down proportionally to the slower apparent velocity of space, NOTHING appears to have changed! If the man was capable of throwing the ball at a speed of one hundred miles an hour when the ship was motionless, to all of those within the ship, the ball still appears to be moving at a speed of one hundred miles an hour! From the perspective of all those within the ship, everything "is as it always was". But this is just the illusion.

In this faster moving frame of reference, the motions of everything have now slowed down proportionally to the motions of everything else. This means that EVERY motion, including all motions within all assorted types and kinds of clocks, now takes place at a slower rate than it did when it was at rest in reference to the earth.

Hence, a clock attached to a wall in the interior of the spaceship now runs slower in reference to a clock on the earth. It runs slower because every motion of every atom within the clock now takes twice as long as it did before. When it used to tick off two seconds, it now ticks off only one second. One hour becomes a half-hour, and 24 hours turns into 12!

[If an atomic clock is launched into space aboard this spaceship, orbits the earth at a high rate of speed, and is then brought back down to the surface; comparing its time to the time on another atomic clock will make it seem as if this clock has run slower. Which it has. However, it was not "time" that was the cause of this "Time Dilation" effect. Instead, it was the slower apparent velocity of *dense and flowing space* that was the culprit. Allowing us to see the real cause of this time dilation experiment that is supposedly used as a proof of Einstein's Theory of Relativity!]

Returning our attention to the spacecraft, because all motions have slowed down proportionally to all other motions, the biological processes within the traveler's body have slowed down too! This means that in addition to the motions of the atoms and molecules within the traveler's body, his very thought processes will also have slowed down proportionally to the slower motions of the atoms within in his body. Since the electric current and chemical reactions within his body have slowed down, his thoughts and perceptions have slowed down, making it seem to him as if nothing within the ship is any different from what it was before!

However, everything *is* different. Motions have not only slowed, but the shapes of everything within the ship are now radically distorted, but amazingly, everything still appears to be normal.

Everything still appears normal because of the greatest optical illusion ever created. If we could see past the illusion we would view what only can be called *THE REAL AND FRIGHTENING VISION OF THE UNIVERSE!* (This startling vision will be revealed in Book two of this three-part trilogy.)

Ch26 THE END OF THE THEORY OF RELATIVITY

The era of the Theory of Relativity comes to a close when it is realized that Albert Einstein's vision of the universe is completely wrong. The Theory of Relativity is based upon the effects of the universe and not the causes.

There are two completely different visions of the universe: the vision of effect, and the vision of cause. The first vision is seen with our eyes, while the second vision is perceived with our minds. And even though each appears real, the first is nothing but an illusion created by the second.

The idea that space is made of nothing, matter is made of something, and time exists as a fourth dimension is totally wrong! Nothing could be further from the truth.

Even though Mr. Einstein's fourth dimension of "space-time" was a brilliant idea, his use of it to explain the length shrinkage and time dilation effects associated with near light velocities was dead wrong. Einstein was close to the truth, but his use of the fourth dimension was more of a metaphysical explanation than a precise mechanical explanation.

Although there is a fourth dimension, it doesn't possess any "time" characteristics. It doesn't somehow create length shrinkage and time dilation effects. Instead, when matter moves, it is the shrinkage of the vortices themselves that are flowing back and forth between three dimensional space and higher dimensional space that are creating the length shrinkage effects. And as can be seen in THE PROOF, it is the slower apparent velocity of *dense and flowing space* that is creating the "time dilation" effects.

Einstein once said, "Imagination is greater than education". A profound insight which is absolutely true! For when everyone is trained alike, everyone thinks alike, everyone reasons alike, and everyone comes to the same conclusions.

This continued way of thought does not find errors, but reaffirms errors from one generation to the next. The only way to break this misleading cycle is to throw away the authoritarian educational training received from others and to use one's own imagination to think in ways no one has ever thought in before.

This was the very way of thinking that launched Einstein upon a voyage of discovery, but never allowed him to reach the "New World". Mr. Einstein's problem was that he tried to incorporate the concept of time into all of his ideas, never realizing that this was the excess baggage of past generations which needed to be discarded before ever trying to make the trip.

Although he was right many times, he was also wrong.

Einstein's use of his imagination allowed him to correctly deduce that the speed of light would be measured the same for all observers everywhere no matter how fast they were travelling. A brilliant deduction! However, because Einstein believed space was made of nothing, he never deduced the principle of the "backdrop of space". Hence, from Einstein's point of view, the motions of everything in the universe were "relative" to the motions of everything else. A situation that appears to be absolutely true for the observations of the planets, stars, and galaxies we see from our perspective as human beings living here upon the Earth. Hence, the Lorentz transformation equations that allow us to calculate the "time differences" between two moving frames of reference are still valid. And even though the "twins paradox", the orbit of Mercury aberrations, and many other observations from the "relativistic" vision of the universe are still real effects, the causes of these effects have nothing to do with the concept of time.

Just as Newton's laws are still applicable even though they were amended by the Theory of Relativity, the Theory of Relativity is still applicable too, even though it is now amended by the Vortex Theory.

However, in the "microscopic" world of the atom, things are very different. The "microscopic" universe possesses a completely different perspective than that seen from the "macroscopic" point of view of the universe.

The view of the universe from inside a proton or an electron is completely different from the relativistic view. Because of these two differences in perspective, there will always be two truths to our viewpoint of the universe. There is the truth of cause and the truth of effect.

The misunderstanding of these two truths has fooled many of the greatest thinkers who have ever lived. Aristotle was fooled. Aristotle believed everything above the orbit of the Moon was unchanging. An observation which from his perspective [and from ours], appears to be absolutely correct! When we look up at the positions of the stars in the sky, they do indeed appear to be forever eternal and unchanging. A mistaken belief that makes his assumption appear to be absolutely true. Indeed, it is a true effect - we actually see it. In fact, from the time we are born until the time we die, nothing appears to have changed in the night sky. We can truthfully witness and testify to this effect in court.

Even so, nothing could be further from the truth. Everything in the sky is constantly changing its position. What we are witnessing and testifying to are only the effects we are seeing from our point of view here upon the earth. Today, we all know that the cause of this effect results from the fact that these stars are so incredibly far away that their actual motions are indiscernible.

Another example of these two contrary truths is seen in the rotation of the heavens. From the viewpoint of every generation up to and including Copernicus, it appeared as if everything was revolving around the Earth. Although the stars do not appear to move as individuals, "en-mass" they appeared to revolve as one group - along with the Sun, Moon, and planets around the Earth. Which is a true observation. However, as before, this is only the effect we are seeing. As we now know, the cause of the effect is being created by the rotation of the Earth itself.

Cause and effect - it crops up again and again in mans observations of the universe. We see an effect and try to assign a cause to it, but many times the causes we assign are completely wrong. But this technicality doesn't seem to bother most people. People need answers, and if one fulfills this need, whether it is right or wrong, the uncertainty is eliminated and men are satisfied.

When their children ask them the same questions they asked their parents, they are happy to be able to give them an answer. Soon the answer becomes part of the collective heritage of the ideas passed on from generation to generation. It becomes a belief and becomes a part of our mythology. The more people who believe it, the more believable it becomes.

In knowing how errors are made and propagated from generation to generation, we now understand Mr. Einstein's error. Like everyone else, he was taught to believe in the erroneous concept of time. Since he believed in time, he believed that the cause of the time dilation effects that occur at near light velocities was "time". However, after the discovery of the Vortex Theory, we can now see that there is a difference between the "effect" of time and the "cause" of time.

Although the "effect" of time - [the phenomenon of time] - appears to be real, it is not being created by "time". Instead, the motions of everything within the physical universe are creating it. However, it must be realized that these motions are themselves a function of the ELASTICITY OF SPACE. A characteristic of space that causes it to move at the same rate everywhere throughout the universe.

This similar rate creates a "synchronous repetition" for harmonic motions. Making all similar motions of matter occur at the same rate everywhere. Therefore, anything, which might change the elasticity of space, will also change the rate at which motions occur, creating the effect of "time dilation". Hence, the intense "gravitational fields" created by the massive regions of less dense space which exists around stars, changes the elasticity of space - making it move slower - creating time dilation effects. Allowing us to finally understand why "gravity" affects time. Answering the last of the enigmas of Relativity. Consequently, in lieu of the above knowledge, the Theory of Relativity is now but another chapter in the history of mankind. An era gone by! An era noted for its nuclear bombs and atomic powered submarines. Another era attributed to the worst and the best which mankind has to offer. An arrogant era where physicists told the people of the world that Einstein's Theory of Relativity was absolutely right, and anybody who disagreed was either uneducated or a fool! Well, at least they didn't burn people at the stake like their predecessors did!

What a time!

Although it is sad to see the end of an era, it is exciting to contemplate the beginning of a new one. An era which promises to be mankind's greatest!

REFERENCES

Editors note: THE END OF THE CONCEPT OF 'TIME' is a revolutionary work containing knowledge unique unto itself and found in no other books in the world. Hence it has few references.

Rucker, Rudy: *THE FOURTH DIMENSION*

Abbott, Edwin A.: *FLATLAND*, New York, Dover Publications, 1953

Besancon, Robert M.: *THE ENCYCLOPEDIA OF PHYSICS*, pages 568-570; and 949-950, Van Nostrand Reinhold co., 1974

Condon, E. U.: *THE HANDBOOK OF PHYSICS SECOND EDITION*, pages 6-162-164, and 2-65-66 McGraw Hill Book Co., 1967

Eisberg, Robert: *FUNDAMENTALS OF MODERN PHYSICS*, pages 9-15 John Wiley and Sons, 1961

Scarre, Chris: *SMITHSONIAN TIMELINES OF THE ANCIENT WORLD*, page 65, Dorling Kindersley, Inc., 1993

Dorthy Michelson Livingston: *THE MASTER OF LIGHT*, A biography of Albert A. Michelson, University of Chicago Press, 1973